Wealth of EXPERIENCE

Wealth of EXPERIENCE

Real Investors on What Works and What Doesn't

The Vanguard Group

Andrew S. Clarke

WILEY

John Wiley & Sons, Inc.

Published by John Wiley & Sons, Inc., Hoboken, New Jersey.
Published simultaneously in Canada.

For general information on our other products, and services, or technical support, please contact our Customer Care Department within the United States at 800-762-2974, outside the United States at 317-572-3993 or fax 317-572-4002.

Wiley also publishes its books in a variety of electronic formats. Some content that appears in print may not be available in electronic books.

For more information about Wiley products, visit our web site at www.wiley.com.

ISBN 0-471-22684-X

Printed in the United States of America.

10 9 8 7 6 5 4 3 2 1

CONTENTS

FOREWORD

Ever since I was in high school, I have coached kids' sports in my free time. After coaching hundreds of boys and girls over the last few decades, I still find it fascinating to participate in the development of young athletes. Many factors contribute to a young athlete's development, including a desire to succeed, innate ability, good coaching, and lots of practice sessions. But good athletes must also be able to learn from experience. And those who make the most progress are the ones who are able to learn from their own successes and failures on the playing field—and from the successes and failures of other players.

In investing, it's also important to learn from experience. You can read all the investment advice books you want—and there are more with every passing year!—but there is no substitute for lessons learned in life. In some cases, those real-world experiences are more valuable than all the investment theory you'd get in any graduate-level finance course.

For example, anyone who was invested in the stock market in 2000–2002 certainly gained a memorable lesson about risk. The Standard & Poor's 500 Index declined –49.15% from March 24, 2000, to October 9, 2002, marking that period as the stock market's deepest and longest downturn since the Great Depression. Most equity investors have been sorely tested by this relentless bear market. Some threw up their hands and fled from stocks to the apparent safety of money markets and bonds.

The valuable lesson to draw from the recent bear market is not that stocks are too risky. Rather, the right lesson is about the value of investing with balance—holding both stocks and bonds to mute the overall volatility of a portfolio. The bear market also demonstrated the wisdom of diversification—spreading one's money across a range of stocks (or bonds) instead of investing in narrow market sectors or in the holdings of a few companies.

Learning about balance and diversification is valuable, but the cost of these lessons was terribly high for some investors. Trillions of dollars in wealth evaporated in the bear market, and many individuals who held concentrated, undiversified portfolios lost so much money that they've had to make changes in their current lifestyle or defer their dreams of retirement.

There's an old saying that experience is the worst teacher because it always gives the test first and the instruction afterward. So how does one get the benefit of experience without suffering all of the hard knocks? One of the best ways I know is to learn from the experiences of others—both the positive experiences and the negative ones. During more than two decades at Vanguard, I've spoken with thousands of shareholders and learned a great deal from them. These are ordinary people—largely do-it-yourself investors—who by dint of focus and discipline have achieved financial security. Their wisdom was a key source for our 2002 book, *Straight Talk on Investing: What You Need to Know*.

For *Wealth of Experience: Real Investors on What Works and What Doesn't*, by my colleague Andy Clarke, we decided to take a systematic look at our clients' experiences. In his research, Andy uncovered many of the same themes that run through *Straight Talk*, namely, that successful investing is largely a matter of constructing a prudent, well-diversified plan that suits your individual goals, time horizon, and risk tolerance and that minimizes your costs—and then sticking to it. Of course, that's easier said than done, given the fads and distractions that can lead an investor astray.

Wealth of Experience is based on comments from 600 Vanguard shareholders who answered a 2002 survey about their investing attitudes, goals, and preferred strategies. These respondents are, again, ordinary people who have accumulated wealth by developing sound investment plans and sticking with those plans through all kinds of markets. They share tips on saving money, advice about how to manage a personal investment program, and some frank and useful confessions about errors they've made over the years. You can learn a great deal from their experiences, and if you apply their lessons to your own investment program, I think you can become a better investor.

In addition to gaining practical tips from this book, you can build your confidence as an investor. Just like the rest of us, these men and women have faced harrowing markets, personal financial challenges, and uncertainty about their ability to make good investment decisions for themselves. They've persevered and learned from their experiences. And they've proved that ordinary people *can* take responsibility for their own financial well-being through disciplined investing. You can too.

John J. Brennan
Chairman and CEO, The Vanguard Group
May 1, 2003

ACKNOWLEDGMENTS

Wealth of Experience is primarily the work of the 600 "What Works" investors who devoted significant time and thought to an 11-page survey about their investment experiences and practices. They deserve our deepest thanks for sharing the insights that made this book possible.

In addition to the investment professionals who provided valuable commentary for *Wealth of Experience*, a number of people had a hand in the manuscript. Rob Grofe created the databases that allowed us to organize thousands of different responses from the "What Works" investors. Holly Fergusson and Kathy Leavesley lent their expertise to creating and carrying out the investor survey. Molly Ruzicka, an editor in Vanguard's Communications group, trained her keen mind and sharp pen on the manuscript, and made it much better. Veteran editorial staffers Marta McCave and Mary Lowe Kennedy shared their customarily excellent ideas along the way. Craig Stock and Mike Hernan, principals in the Communications group, contributed to the project from its conception through the writing and editing process, and team members Nikki Alvanitakis, Jeanene Boggs, Robert Eisenbrown, and Louise DiFilippo led us down the final stretch. Matthew R. Walker, Vanguard's Associate Counsel, helped with contracts and survey issues. Colleen Jaconetti and her colleagues in Investment Counseling & Research and Asset Management and Trust Services—Bruce Freeston, Charles Corrigan, Frank Ambrosio, and Lisa Bianculli—lent invaluable help with financial-planning questions and concepts. Lynne Brady and her team in our Fund Information Services Group—Donna Sanna and Ker Moua—made sure that the statistics used in the book were accurate.

Finally, this book would not exist if Jeremy Duffield, managing director of Vanguard Investments Australia, had not first proposed and then undertaken a similar project Down Under, which was published in 2002 as *Wealth of Experience: Investors Share Their Secrets*. Obviously, we stole his title.

INTRODUCTION

Investing with the 'What Works' Investors

The investment literature is rich with theory. The best works have established a logical and coherent framework that explains the seeming chaos of the financial markets: the interplay between risk and return, the composition of efficient portfolios, and how the price you pay for a share of General Motors stock is influenced by the price of the U.S. Treasury bill and the risk premium demanded by the industry's financiers.

There are also many excellent books—some of them by Vanguard chairman Jack Brennan and Vanguard founder and former chairman John C. Bogle—that serve as a bridge between theory and practice. These books respect, as well as build on, the groundbreaking theoretical work of the past 50 years while giving readers nuts-and-bolts guidance and advice on developing investment programs that can help them reach their financial goals.

Wealth of Experience is written in the tradition of these pragmatic books, but it approaches the task from a different—and unique—perspective. During 2002, Vanguard conducted a survey to study the investment experiences and lessons of ordinary people—people for whom investing is a responsibility, not a career or a hobby. Our findings reinforce the lessons we've learned in the course of 27 years of serving clients: Success in meeting financial goals reflects not specialized training nor sophisticated strategies so much as the consistent application of a few basic principles. Some people benefit from the expertise of professional advisers, including Vanguard's own financial planners and trust officers. Some people go it alone. In both cases, the master keys to investment success have been forged by following a handful of time-honored precepts.

The 'What Works' Survey

The "What Works" survey included responses from 600 Vanguard shareholders. About 80% of them were high-net-worth investors, meaning they have Vanguard assets of more than $250,000. The remaining respondents, or "core" shareholders, hold Vanguard assets of less than $250,000. The high-net-worth investors hold investment portfolios (Vanguard and non-Vanguard assets) worth, on average, about $2 million. The core shareholders have average Vanguard investments and non-Vanguard assets of $641,000. The high-net-worth shareholders tend to be older than the core shareholders, and they have acquired more investment experience.

About 65% of respondents were retired. Male respondents outnumbered female respondents by four to one, but in many cases a man (or woman) answered the survey on behalf of the entire household. The respondents' median age was 65, with 30% younger than 60, 33% aged 60 to 69, and the remainder aged 70 and above.

The survey respondents represent a variety of educational backgrounds: 21% did not graduate from college, 29% were college graduates, and the remainder pursued study beyond college. The group was relatively affluent, with a median annual household income of $149,000: 44% of respondents had household incomes of less than $100,000, and 56% had incomes greater than $100,000.

The "What Works" survey included both *closed-end* questions that could be analyzed statistically (such as "At what age did you make your first investment?") and *open-end* questions (such as "What do you consider your most disappointing investment experience?"). The responses, supplemented by telephone interviews, are the heart of this book. Much of the text, in fact, is quotations, edited only for clarity, from survey responses and conversations with the "What Works" investors. (In some cases, we also omitted the names of particular fund and financial services companies, particularly if the reference was unduly promotional or derogatory.)

Although all the survey participants hold accounts at Vanguard, many also invest elsewhere, including other mutual fund companies and major brokerage firms. We mention this to allay any concern that survey respondents robotically repeated the Vanguard view. They rely on a number of investment providers and sources of information, and their insights reflect a true diversity of thought. In many cases, their advice is similar to the counsel we have long offered investors, but in other instances, these investors have positions at odds with Vanguard's investment beliefs.

The book also includes commentary from Vanguard officers who work with clients on broad financial-planning questions and narrower investment-selection issues. In their day-to-day duties, these Vanguard leaders manage portfolios, prepare investment and estate plans, select advisers for and monitor the portfolios offered by Vanguard, and develop and manage the services that can help our clients to succeed. The perspectives of these officers provide additional insight into the steps that all investors can take to reach their goals.

The Goals of This Book

Wealth of Experience aims to distill the investment wisdom of survey respondents into a simple plan that any investor, novice or expert, can use to enhance his or her prospects for long-term success.

This book also serves to profile the habits and attitudes of investors who have achieved a measure of success during a generation-long revolution in investing that has put most of us in charge of managing our own financial futures. Even if you've already charted a sensible course toward your financial goals, you'll find bountiful learning opportunities here in the accounts of your traveling companions.

Although there's broad agreement on the big things you need to do to manage your investments, it's important to reiterate that these investors hardly speak with one voice. Some never invest in individual stocks; others keep the bulk of their assets in individual holdings. Some dabble in options; others steer clear of anything but fixed income securities. Some investment questions have no right answer, just different trade-offs. In working with clients, the Vanguard leaders/commentators have looked at these tricky issues from both sides of the table, and they provide their thoughts on a number of dilemmas raised by the "What Works" investors.

Lessons of Experience

For the most part, the "What Works" investors' advice is disarmingly simple: Save, make a plan and stick with it, learn about investing, diversify and allocate your assets, monitor your progress, and cut costs and taxes. These and other topics are covered in the first nine chapters of the book, which describe the building blocks of a successful investment program.

Survey respondents haven't been uniformly successful, of course. "Experience is the name everyone gives to their mistakes," in the words of Oscar Wilde, and his observation rings especially true in investing. But some of the survey respondents' most interesting insights come from bad investment experiences. Mistakes can be an effective teacher, and if you learn from someone else's mistakes, you can spare yourself some pain.

In Chapter 10, investors discuss legacy issues, both familial and financial. The topics include charitable giving, estate planning, and the role of families and friends in shaping investment habits. There were dissenting voices, to be sure, but many "What Works" investors considered the task of helping the next generation of investors to acquire financial survival skills to be an important part of their investment programs.

Chapter 11 explores the traits of successful and unsuccessful investors. These themes emerge throughout the book, but they are packaged in a separate chapter because of the importance of aligning your investment approach with your own individual temperament. It may be impossible (and undesirable) to rewire your personality, but everyone can pick up some useful ideas from the habits and traits of people who have succeeded in meeting their financial goals.

In Chapter 12, the book's final chapter, we canonize the "What Works" investors' lessons of experience as eight commandments that can direct you toward your investment goals.

Advice for the Times

We're living through an extraordinarily challenging period in the stock market, one of the longest and deepest downturns in modern financial history. Some of the investors we surveyed described this downturn as their worst investment experience. What makes their counsel so powerful, however, is that these investors haven't had to change their thinking in response to the tough markets. Their advice is timeless. It's the counsel they followed during the overheated stock markets of the late 1990s; it's the advice they followed during the stock market's doldrums of 2000–2002; and it's the advice they'll follow when the markets stage their inevitable recovery.

Several "What Works" investors said that they have been there before. They were investing during the stock market's long, grinding decline from 1973 to 1974. (At that time, bonds collapsed, too, but during the downturn of 2000–2002, bonds produced stellar returns.) They continued to invest through an anemic stock and bond market recovery that didn't gather steam until 1982. But when the rebound came, they were ready. Principles of saving, balance, diversification, and the other lessons outlined in this book put them in a position to achieve their financial goals. Investors who follow the same principles through the current storm will no doubt be able to say the same one day.

Wealth of EXPERIENCE

chapter one
SAVE YOUR MONEY

If you don't save, you can't invest. It's that simple. The 600 investors who responded to our 2002 "What Works" survey were nearly unanimous—and surprisingly forceful—in their opinion that saving is the single most important key to investment success. "This is vitally important: saving today so you can have financial success tomorrow," wrote a middle-aged investor now living overseas. "Be consistent when it comes to saving. Don't touch savings. You don't need to have three TVs, two VCRs. Make do with one of each. A good investor has to find happiness with what's around him. You don't need to purchase material things to be happy."

The simple act of regularly setting aside money outweighs the importance of asset allocation, investment selection, tax management, and every other element of investing. Selecting an appropriate mix of stock and bond funds and cash investments, keeping a lid on costs—certainly, these things are important, and the larger your portfolio grows, the more important they become. But first you need to grapple with the reality articulated by a midcareer executive near Chicago: "You can't invest and grow money that you don't have. There is no better way to build wealth than saving."

A good savings program also compensates for the inevitable mistakes that all investors make. We heard from investors who lost every dime they invested in limited partnerships, risky initial public offerings (IPOs), and oddball tax shelters, often destroying big chunks of their net worth. If regular saving is a habit, however, these mistakes rarely prove fatal.

Saving can provide some emotional benefits, too. Results from the "What Works" survey and from academic research indicate that those who began saving early, as well as those who made it a habit, reported less anxiety about future financial uncertainties: health care costs, retirement income, and stock market declines. Many also got a sense of satisfaction and accomplishment from saving.

Saving is the foundation on which every other investment lesson in this book rests. In this chapter, "What Works" investors recount their efforts to make saving a high priority, including their attitudes toward a practice that, in essence, means forgoing today's wants for tomorrow's needs. The findings of a recent academic study about the role of savings in building wealth are also discussed. This research emphatically corroborates the observations of the "What Works" investors. At the chapter's end, the investors suggest simple steps you can follow to enhance your own savings.

Everyone Can Save More

There are thousands of reasons not to save. Most people are familiar with the general dilemma (if not all the specifics) described by one investor. "At 20 years of age, it's 45 years to retirement, an eternity. Plus there is no way to really know how much you should be saving, because you have no way of knowing how much your investments will earn in 45 years, what the rate of inflation will be, what your lifestyle will be in retirement, and how much you will need to finance it. Then there is competition for your income—family, marriage, divorce, remarriage." There's just not much left to save, and every year there's less, as illustrated by the collective actions of the nation's savers and spenders in Figure 1.1.

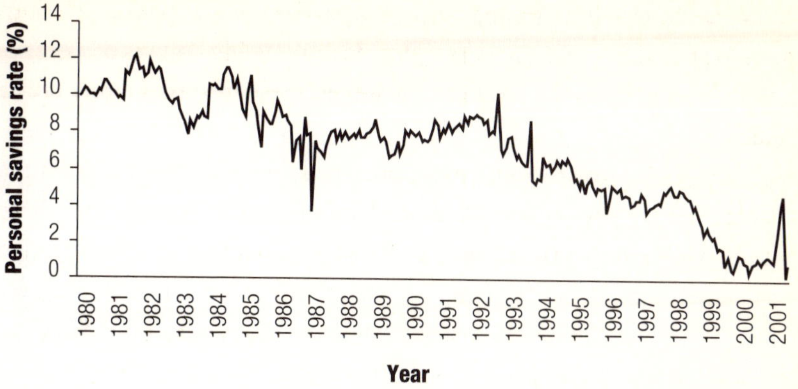

FIGURE 1.1 Americans are saving less.
Source: Federal Reserve Bank of St. Louis.

That's the conventional wisdom, at least. But some "What Works" investors learned a different lesson in their unconventional reality. One Texas investor said his greatest investment experience was "watching my mother save money living on Social Security while seeing a N.Y.C. lawyer friend barely make ends meet on $500K in annual salary. 'Spend less than you earn and invest the rest' is true regardless of the number of zeros in your paycheck." In fact, academic research has shown that people of just about any income level have the means to save their way to impressive levels of wealth. Saving no doubt requires some changes in consumption and behavior, but the notion that most people earn just enough to get by isn't supported by the data.

Steven F. Venti, an economics professor at Dartmouth College, and David A. Wise, a Harvard University economist, recently studied the differences in wealth accumulation for close to 4,000 households with similar lifetime incomes.[1] Even among workers who took home similar-sized paychecks, there were big differences in the amount of wealth accumulated.

Many of those with the lowest lifetime incomes—meaning the sum total of their lifetime paychecks placed them in the bottom 10% of all earners—finished their working lives with zero wealth. Not surprising.

However, about 10% of those low earners accumulated an average of almost $200,000, and a small handful boasted more than $500,000 in wealth.

At the other end of the wage scale, the professors found a number of high earners with very little to show for years of big paychecks. About 10% of these high-income households finished their working years with less than $200,000, though the richest 10% amassed millions of dollars in wealth.

The primary reason for these differences in wealth is simple: saving. Those who saved the most accumulated the most wealth, while those who saved the least wound up with very little. Other factors had minimal bearing on the amount of wealth accumulated. An inheritance from a rich aunt, a costly medical crisis, or even whether a household had children made a relatively small impact on the amount of wealth acquired over a working lifetime.

Neither, surprisingly, did the way those savings were invested. A household's exposure to higher-risk, higher-returning assets such as stocks didn't explain much of the differences in wealth. Venti and Wise concluded that most of the difference between the wealth of those with similar incomes "must be attributed to differences in the amount that households choose to save."[2]

Our survey found that 16% of high-net-worth investors (with Vanguard assets of at least $250,000) who were still in the workforce had household incomes of less than $100,000 a year. That threshold allows for a nice income, but it's by no means a king's ransom. Modest income and immodest wealth don't need to be a contradiction in terms. "It doesn't matter how much you make," a California retiree told us, "it's how much you save."

Modest income and immodest wealth don't need to be a contradiction in terms. "It doesn't matter how much you make," a California retiree told us, "it's how much you save."

A Little Goes a Long Way

You don't have to start big, but it helps to start early. "A lot of people just think, 'Oh, I'll do it later,' " a "What Works" respondent told us. "I remember a quote from [famous investor Warren] Buffett that said something like 'the best savings is early savings.' " The earlier you start, the better your ability to harness the awesome power of compounding—the process by which your savings earn interest, and by which that interest earns interest, and that interest earns interest, and so on. One mark of the unsuccessful investor is "spending too much when you are young, so you don't accumulate enough wealth to invest when compounding would do the most good," observed one respondent. As the saying goes, it's not timing the market, it's time in the market.

Suppose you start saving $100 a month at age 25. You invest the money in a mix of stock and bond funds that returns an average of 8% a year. The results are presented in Figure 1.2. By age 40, after 15 years of investing, your total contributions of $18,100 have increased in value to $35,167. Not bad, but not life-changing money, either.

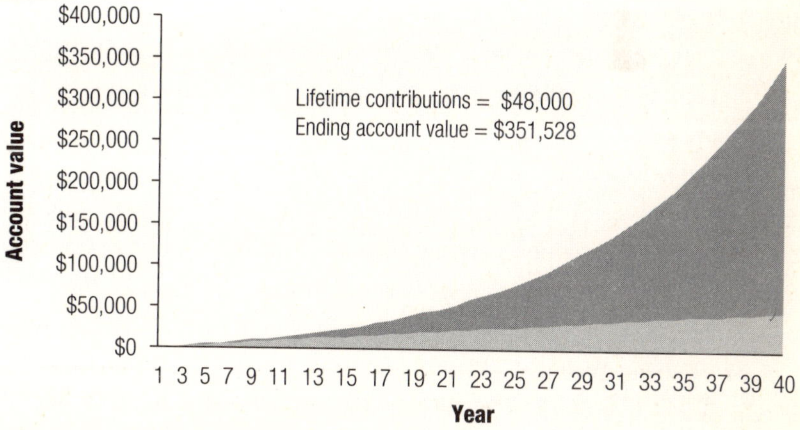

FIGURE 1.2 Time is money.

Source: The Vanguard Group, Inc.

Notes: Monthly investments = $100; annual return = 8%.

From that point on, however, compounding kicks into high gear. The account's 15 years of accumulated interest now represent a large enough pool of assets that earnings on your earnings become real money. The darker mountain chart in Figure 1.2 slopes sharply upward, while the amount of money contributed—the relatively flat slope at the foot of the mountain—continues to creep up at just $100 a month.

After another 15 years, the value of the account has grown to $151,130, while your contributions total just $36,100. And at the end of 40 years, when you reach age 65, the account is worth $351,528—more than seven times your lifetime contributions of $48,000. The mathematical abstraction of compounding provides concrete benefits in the real world. "Get into a regular investment program when you are young," a Midwest investor told us. "The difference in cost between an Accord and a BMW will buy you several nice cars if invested wisely until retirement."

Becoming a Saver

Saving comes easier to some people than to others. Some people we spoke to developed the savings habit in youth, were inspired by a family member, or were shaped by the unique circumstances of their time and place. Others seemed to be natural-born savers, instinctively husbanding resources for the future.

"I was born in 1926, and I remember when the banks closed," one West Coast investor told us. "In the school system, Bank of America had some kind of savings program for kids. I had a small bank account. During the Depression my father was a salesman, and an axle broke on his car, and he took the money out of my account. So it all started with school." During World War II, this investor earned $50 a month in the U.S. Navy, and used $18.75 of it to buy War Bonds. Saving 38% of your income sounds extraordinary today, but people of the same generation told us similar stories. "Saving is a virtue for people of the Depression," another respondent said. "We tried to teach our children to spend wisely. That was different for me. I was taught to save and hang on to it."

Some people were inspired by the example of a family member or the counsel of a public figure. A city worker, now retired, told us, "There are various things in your life that make a life-changing impact. Earl Nightingale was a motivational speaker back in the 1950s and 1960s. He said '10% of what you earn is yours to keep.' Since then, we've always tried to save 10% and give 10% to the church or charities."

This investor's father-in-law was another important influence. "He invested in stocks and bonds every month from the 1950s until his death in 1996. He was just a floor supervisor at Ford Motor Company. He had a modest income, but he was able to leave $1.9 million in his estate."

Sometimes the savings impulse represents a combination of instinct and conscious effort. "In the 1950s, I would mow lawns around the neighborhood. And I would be paid in coins. I would put them in a can and melt candle wax on them, so if I wanted to get at the money, I'd have to boil the coins. It was forced saving."

These savers owe some of their success to chance: the good luck of being born into a family that set a good example, or the paradoxical luck of coming of age during a tough time in the nation's history. But what if you grew up in easier times? Or never learned much about saving from your family or other role models? There are a number of time-tested methods for increasing your savings. You might need to kick some old habits and adopt new ones, but these strategies work precisely because they're not terribly painful. The first step is coming to terms with the anti-savings: debt.

There are a number of time-tested methods for increasing your savings. The first step is coming to terms with the anti-savings: debt.

Dealing with Debt

Debt isn't necessarily bad, but "do not borrow money for anything that does not appreciate in value (education and home)," one investor cautioned. Debt incurred to pay for education should translate into higher earnings, more than compensating for the cost of the loans. Mortgage loans are another big source of borrowing. Few homebuyers can pay cash, but you need a place to live, and as you pay down the loan, you build up equity, a kind of savings, in your home. Plus, home values have tended to appreciate, and Uncle Sam helps you pay the mortgage by allowing you to deduct the interest on your loan from your income for tax purposes.

The most dangerous kind of debt is high-cost revolving, or credit-card, debt. "Pay off all credit cards now!" thundered one "What Works" investor. In 2001, revolving debt approached $700 billion, analogous to a credit-card balance of some $2,500 for every man, woman, and child in the United States. Personal bankruptcies skyrocketed, as debt overwhelmed a record 1.4 million people. Credit-card debt is often incurred to pay for fleeting pleasures or the doodads and gizmos that wind up at the bottom of your closet.

Suppose you borrow $1,000 to buy a digital gizmo. Your credit card charges an annual interest rate of 18%. You make payments of about $30 every month. Four years later, your purchase is paid in full—only it doesn't work anymore. It's sitting at the bottom of a landfill. And the $1,000 you borrowed has wound up costing you $1,400, including financing charges. In economic terms, your costs are even higher. You've lost the opportunity to earn a positive return on that $1,400.

One respondent told us that he thinks of debt as a negative investment. Success is a question of getting on the right side of debt's cash flows. "My grandfather taught me that rather than paying interest to someone else, you should be on the receiving end of interest. I want to be the one who receives the dividends and interest," he said. "My grandfather lent money to people during the Depression and lived on the interest. I've always paid cash for everything, so I've paid very little interest to other people."

Psychological Benefits of Saving

The rewards of a good savings program are more than monetary. "What Works" investors reported that saving provides psychological and emotional benefits, too. More than one-third voiced strong agreement with the statement, "I get a lot of satisfaction from saving for the future." A larger proportion of the high-net-worth investors agreed strongly.

Saving serves primarily to help you meet future material needs, but it can be imbued with emotional value, too, either positive or negative. "My grandparents gave me some money about the time I started high school, and at their suggestion, I put it in a money market account. By graduate school, it was there to help finance costs my stipend wouldn't cover. Also, there were times when it gave me a lot of comfort to know that I'd managed to preserve those gifts, and that I had them for a rainy day."

The "What Works" survey indicated that those who committed themselves to a savings or investment program early in life felt more confident about the future. Table 1.1 shows the percentages of "early savers" and "later savers" who agreed strongly with five statements related to

TABLE 1.1 Psychological Benefits of Saving (Percentage of 'What Works' investors who 'agreed completely')

	Early savers[a]	*Later savers*[b]
Financial success enables me to have freedom and independence to live my life as I desire.	55%	42%
I enjoy managing my money.	43	32
I get a lot of satisfaction from saving for the future.	45	26
I'm in a position to meet all my key financial goals for retirement.	36	16
I worry about having enough money for retirement.	2	13

Source: The Vanguard Group, Inc.

[a]Early savers began investing before age 25.

[b]Later savers began investing after age 35.

the emotional and psychological aspects of saving and investing. On average, early savers had a more positive outlook. Not saving can force you into stressful financial—and emotional—situations. "The average person saves so little that they feel forced into high-risk investments and lottery tickets. They have a need for instant gratification: a 54-inch TV, ocean cruise, fancy new car, two cell phones, and a partridge in a pear tree," said one respondent.

Tips for Saving

The "What Works" investors suggested that everyone can trim his or her daily, weekly, and monthly expenditures to save cash for the future. The respondents were aware of the temptations; they understand the powerful inducements to spend. "It is very easy to buy too expensive a house, too expensive a car, too much of everything at the sacrifice of a regular investment program," wrote a retired professor. Another investor commented: "People don't save. They don't live within their means. Why? They're encouraged to spend by their environment: ads, sitcoms, co-workers. They don't see people living frugally."

The "What Works" investors debunked the notion that thrift means painful sacrifice. "I like to buy good things. I don't buy cheap things, but I wait until they're on sale. We're still very frugal, but not to the point that we deprive ourselves." This man retired early, and now spends his time "trying to repay my debts to society. I've had cancer, and I've started the largest cancer support group in northern California."

Another woman told us, "We invested in IRAs when they first became available, maxed out our 401(k) plans, started medical savings accounts. We took advantage of every savings opportunity. The things that we like to do don't cost a lot of money. Hiking, swimming. That's not why we do them, it just happens that they don't cost a lot of money."

In short, we encountered very few savers writhing in their hair shirts. After all, if you cut back too much on what you truly value, sooner or later your resolve will weaken, and your savings will disappear.

After all, if you cut back too much on what you truly value, sooner or later your resolve will weaken, and your savings will disappear.

After you've identified opportunities for saving, you need to make it a habit. "You must start saving early and get into the habit, or you will spend it on frivolous things," one woman wrote. The "What Works" investors offered a number of other tips.

> "Pay yourself first. That way you don't miss it. You don't know you have it to start with." This is easy to do with retirement plans at work or automatic investment programs at mutual fund companies and brokerages. The money is deducted from your paycheck before you can lay your hands on it. You never see the money, so you'll never miss it.

> "Take all pay raises and invest the raise. Live on a fixed income and invest the raise." If you're getting by on your current income, it should be easy to save the raise.

> "Regular investment should be budgeted just like house payments, electricity, car payments, etc." When you write the bills, make out a check to your savings or investment account. Better yet, have the money deducted directly from your checking account through an automatic investment program.

> "Invest a little as often as you can, and reinvest dividends." Don't spend the dividends paid out by stocks, stock funds, bond funds, or money market funds. Reinvest them in new shares, which will accelerate the rate at which your savings grow.

> "Whatever money I received, I would invest about 10% or 20% of it." Invest extra money such as overtime, bonus pay, income tax refunds, and inheritances.

"Invest every penny you can early. Brown-bag lunch and use the money to purchase great companies." The savings can be substantial, and you might wind up eating better.

First Things First

Just as you must learn to walk before you run, you must save before you can invest. The "What Works" investors made clear that everyone can save more, a claim supported by academic research.

Many respondents cited Warren Buffett, chairman and CEO of Berkshire Hathaway, an insurance giant and investment holding company, as the investor they most admire. Long before Buffett was a famed investor, however, he was a prodigious saver. In *Buffett: The Making of an American Capitalist*, author Roger Lowenstein cataloged Buffett's youthful business ventures: a paper route, golf-ball sales, a pinball-machine rental company. By age 19, from the nickels, dimes, and dollars earned in all these part-time jobs, Buffett "had saved $9,800. That trifling grubstake would be the source of every dollar that Buffett would earn."[3] In 2002, Buffett was worth $36 billion.[4]

You can't hope to compound your savings at Buffett-like rates of return. But his success differs from that of other savers not in kind, only in degree. "Spend less than you earn, and invest the rest." It's that simple.

From Consuming to Saving

by F. William McNabb III

F. William McNabb III is managing director and head of Vanguard's individual and institutional client groups. He joined Vanguard in 1986.

The "What Works" investors have already mastered the single most important element of successful investing: putting aside some of your income so that it can grow and provide for your future.

It's not easy being a saver in the United States. This country is the world's leader in getting folks to buy stuff and, indeed, at getting them into debt to do so. We all get dozens of credit-card offers in the mail every year, and you can't escape advertisements enticing you to use that plastic on, well, you name it. Gadgets and services once considered luxuries have become absolute necessities for many Americans (think cell phones, computer games, restaurant meals, and so on).

So with the odds stacked so heavily in favor of *consuming*, how do you get into the habit of *saving*? It's clear that most of our "What Works" investors don't have superhuman willpower or a lack of appreciation for nice things. Like most successful savers and investors, they save on autopilot. Or, as one of the surveyed investors put it, "Pay yourself first."

Successful investors use payroll deduction to save through retirement plans at work or to buy U.S. Savings Bonds. They use automatic investing plans to put a couple of hundred dollars a month into individual retirement accounts. Or they consider a monthly investment in their bank account or mutual fund to be a bill that they owe to themselves.

If you're a typical American, you'll work for 40 years or more. Even if your annual income averages only $25,000, that means total earnings of more than $1 million. Surely some part of that money ought to be yours to keep and invest so that it can grow for you. I'll close with action steps you can take to begin saving or to save more—the essential ingredient in successful investing. These steps are based on the wise counsel of the "What Works" investors as well as my experience working with shareholders in Vanguard-administered retirement plans.

Action Steps

- **Start.** You may have to start small, but start. You can open a savings account at your bank or credit union with very little cash—probably no more than you have stashed around your house in a coin jar. Don't plan to invest until you've built up your savings to more than $1,000.
- **Go on autopilot.** If you have a savings or retirement plan at work, use it to save painlessly. Even if you can only afford to put aside 1% of your pay at first, go for it. You'll find you can live without that little bit. If your employer matches part or all of your contributions, try to save enough to get the full match—it's like free money. I have yet to meet someone who took part in a 401(k) plan at work for a couple of years who was not pleasantly surprised at how the money built up.

- **Give yourself a raise.** If you get a raise in pay, use at least some of it to boost the percentage you're saving. The key is to start saving the extra money before you get accustomed to spending it. Suppose, for example, that a 35-year-old who gets paid every two weeks increases his or her savings by $40 per pay period. Assuming an average annual return of 7%, the $40-per-pay investment will be worth about $100,000 by the time the investor reaches age 65.
- **Pay down debt.** Owing money on credit-card balances or car loans is negative savings. Paying off that debt, especially high-interest credit-card balances, amounts to saving in two ways. First, it reduces your debt. Second, it reduces the interest building up on that debt. Try to keep your plastic in your pocket. Unless it's a true necessity or you're sure that you can pay off the balance, avoid buying an item on credit. Remember, if you carry a credit-card balance, *you're the one* paying for the frequent-flyer miles, cash rebates, and other incentives that credit-card companies offer for charging it.
- **Use windfalls to help.** If you get a windfall, such as a tax refund, extra pay for working overtime, or money received for a birthday or holiday, try to put at least half of it into savings before you have a chance to spend it.

chapter two

PLAN FOR THE FUTURE

Saving is a condition necessary, but not sufficient, for reaching significant financial goals. The "What Works" investors told us that "the fortitude to stick to a proven plan," some combination of "research, planning, and guts," and "a willingness to set goals and a plan to meet them" were qualities required to transform the humble saver into the successful investor.

A well-conceived plan, said these investors, can be a powerful ally as you strive to reach your personal financial goals. Not only does a plan define what you need to accomplish, but it can also help you make midcourse corrections when the financial markets spring their inevitable surprises—adjustments that some respondents were contemplating as the stock market continued to tumble in summer 2002.

This chapter explains how a plan helps you meet your goals. Without a plan, you may be wandering blind. "I had no goal, and as a result I was susceptible to sales pitches, and I made knee-jerk investment decisions," wrote a Minnesota retiree. The "What Works" investors cataloged the basic elements of a plan and offered advice on designing a program that you can stick with through good times and bad. After all, it does no good to chart a course that looks great on paper but proves untenable in the rough-and-tumble of the financial markets.

Setting Goals

The essence of a plan is your financial goals. An investor in the Southwest noted that one trait of successful investors was "having a long-term realistic plan to meet a specific goal, then sticking with it forever." Every other element of your plan, such as how you invest and how much you invest, will be shaped by the goals you hope to reach.

Academic research corroborates the importance of having both a goal and a plan to meet that goal. In the savings research reviewed in Chapter 1, Venti and Wise asked people whether they had a goal, and if so, whether they had a plan to achieve it. In answer to the question, "Thinking over the past 20 or 30 years, did you have some target or planned level of saving?" only 23% of respondents said yes. But that group of households accumulated higher levels of wealth than did those without a goal. To Venti and Wise's follow-up question, "If yes, did the plan include trying to save something out of each paycheck?" 92% of respondents said yes. They wound up with significantly higher levels of wealth than did the minority who approached the task more sporadically.[1]

"What Works" investors have tried to reach all the typical financial goals. Table 2.1 shows that accumulating assets for retirement was the highest priority, with "general savings for the future" a distant second.

TABLE 2.1 Investing Goals (Percentage of 'What Works' respondents who described selected goals as 'extremely important')

	Total (%)	*Core (%)*	*High-net-worth (%)*
Saving for retirement	47	57	45
General savings for the future	28	34	27
Avoid or reduce taxes	19	18	20
Current income	18	14	19
Building an estate to leave for heirs	12	12	13
Children's/grandchildren's education	10	14	9

Source: The Vanguard Group, Inc.

Although you can't make a plan without a goal, the goal itself can be somewhat vague. As you develop other parts of your plan, you'll be forced to bring your objectives into sharper focus. "What Works" investors described a range of goals, from the specific to the general.

> "When first starting, I wanted to give all of our family a good education and then set enough aside for retirement. Our five children have a college education, which their mother and I did not have the opportunity to pursue. They are all doing well, and we are very proud. Now we are retired and are enjoying the fruits of our investments in a variety of instruments. I have always followed a plan of diversity into many areas and this has served us well."

> "I had a goal in the year 1962 to have $32,000 for my retirement. Since then, I found I had surpassed that figure and now have $1.5 million invested for retirement."

> "I invested for retirement and tax savings. By investing in my husband's Keogh, IRAs, and 403(b) plan to the limit, I reached the limit for tax savings."

> "At first, I did not have a goal in mind. In fact, I used investing as a form of educational gambling. After a couple of years, I decided that investing for the long term was more rewarding and important."

> "My goal was just to save for a rainy day. I began saving very early, and as my financial position improved over the years, so did the amount I thought I needed for a rainy day. I guess you could say I progressed from preparing for a slight drizzle to preparing for a hurricane. Any money I was able to put into investments for retirement or children's education was secondary to emergency money."

"I began saving very early, and as my financial position improved over the years, so did the amount I thought I needed for a rainy day. I guess you could say I progressed from preparing for a slight drizzle to preparing for a hurricane."

"To have an adequate retirement program to support myself and a wife who is 16 years younger than I am. Goal was to have $8 million upon retirement, and exceeded that goal."

"To save regularly; to live within means; to save for our children's higher education; to save for a dream house when we retired. We did save fairly regularly. We only went into debt for our mortgage (and accelerated its amortization). We financed children's education through graduate school. We bought our dream house upon retirement."

"I was saving for grad school. It was real easy: adding the equivalent of my monthly rent to a money market fund every month. Since rates were very high, that was a more than sufficient return, with no principal risk to potentially delay my planned matriculation."

"The goal was to build wealth and the feeling of no-worry independence that goes with it; not great wealth, but comfortable enough. At age 62, I felt I had enough to stop working for a living and do something more leisurely (some people call it 'retiring')."

"My serious investing started in 1986. The goal I set was to invest my retirement money in such a way that my family would live comfortably and that, hopefully, I would go to the great beyond leaving behind at least what I started with on retirement or preferably some reasonable gain. A modest approach in some views, but it works for me, and I've succeeded so far, except for the effects of the current downturn, which hasn't helped sustain the gains. Hopefully history will repeat itself, and the upturn will be effective before a final accounting is made."

"Although one can never predict needs with total accuracy, I tried to estimate future needs for retirement based on the most conservative assumptions. I had no definite time line for achieving my goals, but with a lifetime of conservative spending habits, I was able to watch net worth grow to the point that the original goals were surpassed."

"My purpose in investing was always to gain financial independence for my wife and me. I always believed that, if we saved as much of our earnings as possible and did not make foolish investments, our goals would be met, although I was not as specific in defining the goals as I could have been."

How Much Is Enough?

The next piece of your plan is figuring out what your goal will cost. Expenses such as college tuition are easy to estimate. You know what it costs today, and history suggests that it will probably increase faster than the rate of inflation. Other estimates are trickier. "I do have this feeling in the back of my head that there's this target amount of money we should have that would cover our needs," said a woman in her mid-50s whose primary investment goal is saving for retirement. "I would feel much more secure if we knew that if we had $800,000 or $1 million, and assumed a modest rate of return, we could meet our expenses. But of course the world doesn't work like that. Expenses go up."

When retirement is a distant prospect, it's hard to imagine what your future expenses will be. What standard of living will you have grown accustomed to by the time you leave the workforce? Your expectations and needs at age 65 are likely to be different from your expectations and needs at age 25. But you can make general estimates about what you'll need to spend on food, housing, and other expenses in the future. A ballpark figure is enough to help you lay the foundation of a sensible plan, as illustrated by the approach of some "What Works" investors.

> "At 23, I decided I needed $6,000 a year at 65 and Social Security. This was 1955, and I was earning first lieutenant pay in the Air Force, about $6,600 a year." (An aside: It would take $39,560 in 2001 to purchase the same goods and services that could be bought with just $6,000 in 1955. Prospective inflation is an important influence on the amount of money you'll need in the future.)

> "My goal was just to make money. Only later did I realize that this could become my main retirement vehicle. Starting in 1992, I concentrated on growing my portfolio. I was looking for an amount that would guarantee me an annual income of $50,000 to $60,000. From 1992 to 2000, I steadily progressed toward that goal."

> "I wanted to retire at roughly 60, and I wanted to have enough money. I wanted to have about $600,000 or $700,000."

> "To achieve retirement income on a monthly basis [equivalent to] 80% to 90% of working income. Except for past year, this goal has been achieved."

> "My goal was to be able to retire at age 55 if I wanted to, at about the same income per year that I was making at age 55. I kept annuity-type charts to assess progress."

> "My goal was to save enough assets so that I would have income, including Social Security, of $90,000 a year at retirement."

"Attain net worth of $2 million by age 65. Then work and play until health runs out. Invade principal only when necessary."

"My goal was to reach $1 million. I calculated on index cards, which were all displayed on my desk, how many shares I would need. I always tried to purchase more shares than I calculated I would need."

"My goal was to have $600,000 before retirement. I had close to $900,000 and managed to double that during the period between 1997 and 2000. Like most others, I was hurt during the market decline since March 2001. I lost about 60% over that period and used up another 20% for living expenses."

This last account is a scary story, but the percentages suggest that this retired investor from the upper Midwest should still be in the range of his original goal of $600,000. If his assets peaked at $1.8 million (his $900,000 portfolio doubled in value between 1997 and 2000) and then lost 60% of that figure to the stock market decline, the portfolio would be worth $720,000. If he spent 20% of the remainder on living expenses, his assets would still total $576,000 in early 2002. Indeed, this investor believed he was still in a position to meet all of his key financial goals for retirement. There's no magic formula for estimating what you'll need, but many financial services companies provide tools to help you make an estimate. As a start, you could do worse than simply roughing out a target on the back of an envelope.

Suppose you estimate that when you retire, you'll need $30,000 a year in investment income to supplement Social Security in order to maintain your desired standard of living. Vanguard research suggests that, historically at least, you could withdraw 3% to 4% of a well-diversified portfolio's assets every year, bumped up annually for inflation and with an allowance for taxes, with a relatively low risk of running out of cash.

If you want $30,000 a year over, say 40 years, with annual adjustments for inflation, you'll need to accumulate a portfolio of roughly

$550,000, according to a Vanguard analysis based on the financial markets' historical returns. If you have a short life expectancy, or believe you can earn returns high enough to support a higher withdrawal rate, say 5%, you'll need to save less. But be careful: If you come up short, you'll be in a tough spot.

The Rule of 72

"I would share with people the Rule of 72 (how much it would take to double your money if interest rates remained the same)," wrote one man who reported making his first investment at age 7. Several "What Works" respondents seconded this suggestion.

The Rule of 72 tells you how long it will take to double your money at a given rate of return. For example, if you expect to earn 7% a year on average, divide 72 by 7. Your investment will double in value about every 10 years. If you earn 10% a year, your money will double about every 7 years. Earn 3%, and your money will take 24 years to double in value.

Developing a Strategy

Once you have a goal, and an idea of what it will cost, you can develop a strategy to reach it. One investor described the early stages of his plan: "I knew that my interests would be in volunteer or nonprofit areas. I would not have a high income, and therefore in order to accumulate wealth, I would need to save something." He started with a goal. He hadn't yet calculated a price tag, but he had the beginnings of a strategy, which over time developed into a more detailed plan that today allows him to pursue these interests while preserving assets accumulated for his children's education.

A veteran of several corporate layoffs said: "The realistic view of how people's value in corporations is getting shorter made me recognize how much money you would need at a relatively young age. And the only way it was going to get done was saving and investing. You can't save your way to what you need. You've got to invest." Among this investor's various goals was building a financial cushion for life in what he saw as a changed workplace. "I was laid off for six months last year. I was investing during that time. I can't imagine what it would be like if you didn't have any money."

Figuring out a strategy for reaching your goal involves two variables: (1) How much you can save and (2) how much your savings can earn. The second factor depends on how you invest your money and how those assets perform. "My goal is to retire by 55 with sufficient funds to live in the style I'm accustomed to. My projections are based on my savings rate and a 10% return on investment," explained one investor.

It's hard to estimate the markets' future returns, particularly those of the stock market, but these investors emphasize the importance of setting realistic goals for returns. Oddly enough, even those who have experienced extraordinary success recommended having modest expectations. One investor told us that his most successful investment experience was "holding stock in RJR Nabisco when it was acquired in a leveraged buyout." His conclusion? "The lesson I learned was that windfalls such as the RJR deal are largely luck, and that I should not plan on returns beyond historical averages."

As the following comments attest, many of the "What Works" investors focused more on setting their savings rates—a factor within their control—than on how high a return they might earn.

> "My goal was to save regularly, at least 15% of my salary per year. I did very well saving."

> "My first goal was to establish a savings program. Investing a small pension (from being wounded in World War II) in a mutual fund that would take $10 a month at the time was the starting point."

> "At that time, I did not have a dollar goal, but I have a long-range viewpoint about everything. I wanted to save a significant amount. I did not use a budget; I decided on a fixed percentage of my salary to save and had this deducted from my paycheck. I

never withdrew any of this. At times of need, I would borrow money instead. I am surprised that more people do not use this technique to save money. It is a simple matter of commitment—that is, I will live on 90% of my gross salary, or 95%, or whatever."

"We saved 30% to 60% of gross earnings always."

When you combine your savings rate with a reasonable expected rate of return, it's a simple matter of checking the compound interest tables to figure out how long you'll need to reach your goal. The financial markets offer no guarantees, but determining how long it will take to accumulate a given sum if you save *X*% of your earnings and receive a return of *Y*% on those savings is straightforward mathematics.

Suppose you place your savings in a bank account paying 2% a year. You save 10% of your annual income of $50,000, and you've estimated that you'll need to save $500,000 to fund your retirement. You'll need 55 years of steady saving to accumulate that sum. You can reduce that period by saving more (the safest option) or by pursuing a higher return (a riskier, but for most people, necessary option). If you double your savings rate to 20%, you cut the period down to 35 years. And if you can also boost your average return to 5%, you knock it down to 26 years.

"Be patient. Save and invest all you can. Be realistic. A 5% to 7% return is probable, going forward," estimated one investor. Table 2.2 illustrates the interplay between savings rates and returns, including the 5% to 7% estimated by this investor. The table shows the number of years it takes to accumulate a nest egg equal to ten times your annual salary. If you save 10% of your annual income, and returns are 7%, your assets will be equal to ten times your current salary in 30.7 years. Save 15%, and you'll accumulate that same amount in just 25.6 years. But if returns amount to 5%, you'll need to save 20% of your income to reach that same target within the same period.

If your investment returns are weaker—or stronger—than you anticipate, working with a plan can help you determine whether a midcourse (or later) correction is in order, as the following investors found.

TABLE 2.2 Years Necessary to Accumulate Assets Equal to Ten Times Your Current Salary at Various Rates of Savings and Return

Savings rate	*Return on savings* 5%	6%	7%	8%	9%	10%
5%	49.1 years	44.0 years	40.0 years	36.8 years	34.2 years	31.9 years
10%	36.7	33.4	30.7	28.5	26.7	25.2
15%	30.1	27.6	25.6	24.0	22.6	21.4
20%	25.7	23.8	22.2	20.9	19.8	18.8

Source: The Vanguard Group, Inc.

"I did not plan for a guaranteed income stream at retirement, but expected to live on a 6% to 8% return from the market. I never anticipated three down years and a 30% loss of capital. I should have set aside enough money in bonds or guaranteed return investments to cover retirement expenses."

"I wanted to semi-retire by age 50. I did so. The last few weeks have been painful and made me doubt the equity market. Even though I invest only in broad-based market index funds, the excessive valuations of tech and other large-cap stocks have caused some pain. I don't plan to bail out, but I may reallocate more often than annually, as I have in the past."

"My goal was to retire, and it was going along good until I got hurt on the job and was terminated. I was able to get a cash settlement and invested it. I didn't have as much money as I planned, but am sure glad I invested as I did."

Keep Your Eyes on the Plan

You'll need some tools to put your plan in place—namely, the various investment vehicles that allow you to build a portfolio. But using those tools effectively requires a little study. In the next chapter, "What

Works" investors share their ideas on learning about investing. Then in Chapters 4 and 5, they get down to the nuts and bolts of transforming your savings into an investment portfolio. But first, some final thoughts from respondents about your plan.

> "A successful long-term strategy accounts for market ups and downs, and successful investors resist the temptation to deviate from their plan."

> "The market can be very volatile. Have a long-range plan and stick to it. Don't make big decisions based on short-term results."

> "Develop a sound investment plan that suits you, and stick with it. That means educate yourself! Edson Smith, a financial writer for the *Boston Herald* in the '50s, was a conservative investor, and his mantra was, 'Be content to grow rich slowly.' "

> "Determine your goal, pick a strategy to achieve it, and stick to that strategy. The most achievable goal is to earn an average market return. You can do this by diversification. If you want to take a chance on getting rich, buy a few individual stocks, but realize you will probably go broke. If you cannot stick to a strategy, but are subject to knee-jerk reactions, you should get a professional to manage your investments."

> "Read a book for beginning investors to gain an understanding of the types of investments. Write a financial plan (script only) that includes a long-term vision for what your investments are to achieve, strategies to achieve that vision, criteria individual investments must meet (i.e., must be in a liquid market, must have a predictable maturity date, must have predictable dividend or interest payments, do not have any money that is needed within the next ten years invested in equities). Assemble records from all of your financial resources, and determine what must be

done to achieve your plan. Don't try to be a 'winner.' Continually chasing new investments to achieve the greatest returns will make you a loser in the long run, and you will never achieve your vision. Let others do the boasting, and just be patiently satisfied that you will win in the long run."

"Continually chasing new investments to achieve the greatest returns will make you a loser in the long run, and you will never achieve your vision. Let others do the boasting, and just be patiently satisfied that you will win in the long run."

A sound plan is critical to achieving your investment goals. Although the basic elements of a good plan are simple, living it may not be. When times get tough, keep your eyes on the plan.

The Pieces of a Plan

by Duane D. Cabrera

Duane D. Cabrera, a principal and manager of Vanguard's Personal Financial Planning group, works with clients to develop in-depth investment, retirement, and estate plans. Mr. Cabrera, a Certified Financial Planner, joined Vanguard in 1996.

Creating a financial plan is analogous to planning a vacation. Most people wouldn't just jump in the car and start driving without a few things planned in advance: where they're going, how much money they need, and how long they plan to stay. When it comes to investing, however, this approach is all too common. People prepare for retirement by just jumping into a mutual fund. Contrary to what most people think, the planning process probably has a bigger impact on your ability to meet your financial goals than the amount of your financial resources. There are people who make lots of money but still don't meet their financial goals, so the extent of your resources is just part of the picture.

Setting Goals

The first step in making a plan is to set goals. Too many people dismiss this step as a sideshow, but in reality, it's the main event. Setting goals defines the entire planning process. When setting goals, try to be general about it—get too specific right away and you can easily be discouraged by the seemingly large amounts of money you need. Also, obsessing over the details can sap your motivation. Not many people would describe their vacation plans as "spending $300 per night at a four-star hotel for six nights and seven days." They want "to go to the Bahamas, sit in the sun, and relax." Several "What Works" investors mentioned goals that can be helpful at this stage of the planning process: "Save for a dream house"; "[have] no-worry independence"; "stop working . . . and do something more leisurely." These general objectives can serve as a constant reminder of why you are sacrificing today to meet your goals in the future.

Once you've defined the big-picture goals, you need to fill in the details. Make your goals specific, measurable, and realistic. At this stage, the more specific the goal, the better your ability to assess your progress. People often avoid setting specific goals because it gives them more latitude if things change in the future. Unfortunately, that latitude is the enemy of discipline. And discipline is critical to following through on your financial plan. In fact, though several "What Works" investors seemed to be missing specific, measurable targets, they still appeared to reach their general goals because, even without such targets, they stayed disciplined about saving and investing.

The Price Tag: A Map, Not a Destination

Evaluating the cost of reaching a goal is probably the most difficult step. You're making assumptions about the unpredictable future, and many people simply say, "Why bother?" It's important to realize that these estimates are not meant to be a specific answer such as "You'll need $654,398.73 to finance 23.5 years in retirement." They do, however, give you some perspective about what you need to accomplish. Vanguard.com and many other investment-related Web sites include calculators that can help you develop an estimate.

Picture yourself driving in an unfamiliar place with no map, no street signs, and no one to ask for directions. Which way should you go? Every direction seems as wrong (or right) as the next. If you have a map, you have a better sense of how far you've gone and of how to get to where you are going. But even with a map, several paths may lead to the same place. In a financial plan, the dollar assumptions are there primarily to set you in the right direction and help you stay on course to reach your goals.

After the Plan, the Strategy

Once you know where you want to go, you need to develop a strategy to get there. The key is to find one that works for you. Although the investors in our survey had different approaches, they shared a few things in common. Whether the strategy was to save 15% of all income or to save $10 a month, they followed a consistent, automatic approach to saving—automatic contributions to their 401(k) plans, regular investments deducted from their bank accounts—that imposed some discipline on their plans. Too often, lack of the discipline needed to stick with a plan gets in the way of attaining your goal. It's all too easy to find other ways to spend your money. By building automatic savings mechanisms into your plan, you make sure that the discipline is there.

A final, critical step is picking your investments. Beware: The best-laid financial plan can be ruined by poor investment selection. This was an area where some of the "What Works" investors struggled (see Chapters 4 and 5 for lessons learned as respondents selected investments to implement their plans).

Picture Your Goals and Put Them on Paper

Ultimately, you can say that you are on track or that you need to make changes only if you've taken the time to clarify and write down your financial goals. One thing I'd add is that some people tend to feel that if they put a financial plan in place and do not "hit the numbers" they had projected, they have failed. The reality is that you will never hit the numbers exactly, but that's only to be expected. No one can predict with absolute accuracy at all times how the markets will perform. That's OK. Most "What Works" investors said they were over or under their original goals, but the plans still served their purpose as a point of reference that kept them headed in the right direction over time.

Action Steps

- Identify your general goals.
- Fill in the details: your time horizon, the price tag, and standards for measuring your progress. Use calculators at Vanguard.com and other investment-related Web sites to estimate the cost of your goals.
- Develop a savings and investing strategy that works for you. Use an automatic savings plan to ensure discipline.
- Select the investments for your plan.

chapter three

LEARN THE SECRETS OF SUCCESS

After you've been investing for a while, the whole thing seems simple. Like some of the "What Works" investors, you may be able to condense a lifetime of investing experience into a few short syllables.

- "Diversify. Understand what you own and why you own it. Have a goal and manage to it."
- "Buy and hold."
- "Use index funds."

When you're just getting started, however, investing can seem complicated, a frenetic activity demanding special expertise and hair-trigger reflexes. "Almost all media, even the very best newspapers and television programs on investing, feed into the idea of speculation," noted one investor with almost three decades of experience in the financial markets. "It is very hard to distance oneself from it."

Until you get an education in the basics, you won't recognize that investing has just about nothing to do with television footage of frenzied traders on the floor of the New York Stock Exchange and everything to do with the simple principles espoused by our survey respondents.

These investors identified two basic approaches to acquiring the knowledge and skills needed to invest successfully: (1) doing it yourself or (2) working with a trusted adviser. Both approaches have advantages and drawbacks, and both require at least some self-study. The do-it-yourselfers and those who work with a professional offered advice to those considering either path.

Getting an Education

"A successful investor has a very good knowledge base which he keeps up-to-date. He has a well-defined investment plan, and he has the nerves of steel to stick with it," said a respondent from Maryland. Another noted that successful investors "are willing to learn." And the learning never ends: The tax code mutates. Your goals change. In January 1997, the U.S. Department of the Treasury issued its first inflation-protected securities (TIPS), a fixed income instrument whose value is designed to keep pace with inflation. This development sent even seasoned investors back to the books. As we were preparing *Wealth of Experience* for publication, President George W. Bush unveiled an array of tax proposals with far-reaching implications for investors.

As shown in Table 3.1, "What Works" respondents rely on a number of sources to inform themselves and keep up with current developments. News is not education, however, and most personal finance magazines

TABLE 3.1 Major Sources of Financial News and Information Used by 'What Works' Investors

	Total (%)	*Core (%)*	*High-net-worth (%)*
Financial page of the newspapers	48	45	49
The Internet	19	22	18
Magazines	14	15	14
Television	12	8	13
Radio	4	5	4

Source: The Vanguard Group, Inc.

devote little space to the basics. Respondents indicated that investment management companies can be important allies in your pursuit of an investment education. Of course, educational materials provided by an investment manager may be created with a marketing goal in mind, but in the best circumstances a brokerage or mutual fund company can provide clear, candid information about investment planning and the costs, risks, and potential rewards of a particular investment.

Investors told us that the quality of an investment provider's educational materials plays an important part in their decision to invest with a particular company (Table 3.2). Almost one-third of respondents rated educational services ("helping you to be a smart investor") as "extremely important," ranking somewhat below mission-critical factors, such as costs and the ease of doing business with a firm, but above the industry's often highly touted features, such as online capabilities or financial research. These priorities are sensible but nevertheless surprising. It's as if a restaurant diner said that the availability of nutritional information were more important than the availability of dessert.

Education pays, and lack of it can cost. A 45-year-old investor with assets of more than $1 million told us about losing $1 million in options.

TABLE 3.2 'What Works' Investors' Priorities in Selecting an Investment Company (Percentage responding 'extremely important')

Low costs	66%
Excellent customer service	55
Easy to do business with	52
Superior fund performance	46
Helping you to be a smart investor	29
Emphasizing long-term investments	26
Leader in the industry	26
Breadth of services and fund offerings	22
Online capacities	16
Providing investors with financial research	15
Recommendation from financial professional	7
Recommendation from friend, relative, or co-worker	5

Source: The Vanguard Group, Inc.

He believed the loss could have been averted if he or his adviser had understood the situation. "I wanted to get out," he said. "I asked for some help from the financial adviser. He knew little but acted as if he knew a lot. He gave me bad advice. I learned to trust myself. I am a better investor for the experience. And have done well because of my efforts. It feels good—real good."

Another investor with substantial assets said his worst investment experience was "using a financial adviser to roll over a 401(k) plan after leaving a job. He put us into an investment that at the time we did not understand and were locked into for a long period of time (an annuity). The mistake could have been avoided if we were not so afraid of making a mistake ourselves and if we had taken the time to research what was available to us. The lesson learned was not to invest in anything we do not understand."

An Investing Curriculum

So how do you educate yourself? Most "What Works" investors followed a course of self-study that included not only information from financial services providers and the media but also books, discussions with knowledgeable investors (not always easy to identify), and time spent in the school of hard knocks. At some point, many have worked with a professional. Today, roughly one-fourth of the investors in our survey retain an adviser in some capacity (Table 3.3).

TABLE 3.3 How 'What Works' Investors Make Investment Decisions

	Total (%)	*Core (%)*	*High-net-worth (%)*
Make own investment decisions	76	71	77
Work with financial adviser to make investment decisions	22	24	21
Have financial adviser make decisions	1	3	1

Source: The Vanguard Group, Inc.

A good adviser brings a broad and deep understanding of investments and planning to the task of helping you achieve your unique goals. The comments of some respondents painted a grim picture of advisers, but their complaints mainly concerned salespeople, not advisers who can help clients develop sensible plans to meet their financial goals. Unfortunately, industry jargon makes it difficult to distinguish between the two. The hard-driving salesman who calls to pitch stocks during your dinner often identifies himself as an adviser, but he has no interest in your investment program, just in generating a transaction. And his tips may be worse than worthless. Ultimately, many "What Works" respondents echoed the comments of a Minnesota investor who had soured on the tipsters: "They don't know any more than you do."

In some situations, professional help is a must. Estate planning can be so complex, especially for investors with significant assets, that it's foolish to go it alone. About one-third of our high-net-worth respondents have retained the services of a professional for estate planning (Table 3.4). Professional help can also be critical to prudent retirement planning, that is, devising a strategy for spending your assets while minimizing the risk that you will run out of cash. Such an analysis requires sophisticated financial modeling skills and heavy-duty number crunching.

TABLE 3.4 Use of Financial Planning Services by 'What Works' Investors

	Total (%)	*Core (%)*	*High-net-worth (%)*
Estate planning	28	21	30
Investment planning	21	25	20
Retirement planning	17	26	15
Ongoing advisory service	15	13	15
Trust services	11	7	11

Source: The Vanguard Group, Inc.

Working with Advisers

The experiences of "What Works" investors suggest that accumulating wealth for retirement or other major goals can be accomplished through the application of a few basic principles. Some people manage their wealth with the help of a professional and benefit from the adviser's counsel and planning. But some respondents believe they were led astray by aggressive salespeople masquerading as counselors.

The most common complaint was that sales-oriented advisers put their interests ahead of the investor's. This conflict of interest can be most pronounced in relationships with brokers and advisers who are compensated by commission, which can lead to an emphasis on fee-generating transactions rather than on long-term planning. The more the adviser sells (whether or not the trading is in your best interest), the more he or she earns. Indeed, in March 2002, Stanley O'Neal, now CEO of Merrill Lynch, America's most prominent brokerage, told *Money* magazine: "Making sure that the interests of the client, the financial adviser and the overall business are in alignment is a very, very complicated process. I can tell you that I've never dealt with a more complex topic than financial adviser compensation."[1] "What Works" investors found that this conflict can sometimes be resolved in a way that serves the interests of both sides, but sometimes not.

> "I unfortunately listened to a broker from [major brokerage firm] who sold me three limited partnerships after the market crash in 1987. I lost most of the money in two of them, but a legal suit won on the third ended up well, luckily. I felt badly used by that broker (who was a friend of a friend!) and stupid to have believed her."

> "I telephoned a broker friend whom I respected and asked to make a purchase of bonds of three companies I liked. He returned the call the next day and related his bond department manager's suggestion that I purchase other bonds at a 3% lower

interest rate because the bonds he wished to sell were stronger. They probably were, but the bonds I preferred have done well. I took his advice and made the purchase he suggested and later learned that the $60,000 bonds were a new offering, and that the sales commission for brokers was much greater than on the bonds I wanted."

"I do some volunteer work for the AARP, preparing people's tax returns. One woman had three pages of brokerage transactions. I only recognized one company in that list. The broker was the one making all the money."

"While still working, I attended an investment seminar at a local college. During a follow-up interview with the speaker, I allowed myself to be talked into a small portfolio. Long-term returns were disappointing, and I found later that the recommended investments paid extremely high commissions to the broker."

"Many years ago, when we had begun to accumulate assets and were somewhat inexperienced, we decided to entrust a professional money manager with our investments. We knew this man, and his credentials were impeccable, but the outcome was anything but stellar. When he called in December to tell us he had a 'nice loss' for us, we knew it was time to take back control of our investments. Lesson: No one cares as much about your money as you do."

That's the bottom line. No one else has to provide for your needs in retirement or put your children through college. A clear message from the "What Works" investors is that whether you oversee your own investments or work with a professional, the ultimate responsibility for reaching your goals is yours. This realization can prompt a little soul-searching. One woman in her late forties, with more than a quarter century of investment experience, echoed the words of the previous respondent when she told us that the mark of a successful investor was "a willingness take responsibility for results. Nobody cares as much about your money as you do, no matter how much you pay them (or how much they tell you they care). That takes some work!"

"Nobody cares as much about your money as you do, no matter how much you pay them (or how much they tell you they care)."

Even if you retain a professional, you'll need to do some research to find an adviser who can best meet your needs. Several respondents sidestepped the industry's booby traps and developed a relationship with a trusted adviser whose services proved invaluable.

> "I inherited a small sum of money from my dad. I was working with an insurance agent who strongly advised me to keep the money in a conservative, safe investment. I didn't understand at the time, but he was wise and highly ethical. He was trying to protect me. I was very 'green,' and he could have put me in highly unsuitable investments. I didn't make a lot of money, but I didn't lose anything. I am grateful for his integrity."

> "As I approached retirement, I sought the advice of a well-recommended financial adviser. We worked up a portfolio plan for the disposition of my soon-to-be-received retirement and profit-sharing funds. We chose a well-diversified group of [mutual fund company] funds, which have performed well since

my active retirement. Lesson: Don't try to do it alone. Seek qualified financial advice."

Our respondents offered insight on identifying a good adviser. Just as there is no easy way to identify a good doctor or lawyer, however, finding a good adviser demands a combination of objective and subjective judgment. Some investors counseled:

"Seek the advice of a certified financial planner, preferably one who works on a fee basis with no ties or specific products."

"I learned to deal with a limited number of sources and carefully analyze their recommendations for myself."

"I followed the advice of an investment adviser to allocate my 401(k) across the possible choices of investment vehicles. While everything is down over the past several months, I have been losing more than I have been adding, including my company's matching funds. Even good advice can result in periods of significant loss. I'll get more advice to determine when to readjust."

"Find a guy to trust, but don't turn your back if money's involved."

These experiences suggest general lessons. You can benefit by working with capable people who understand your goals and how to achieve them. Equally important is finding an adviser whose compensation and incentives don't stand in the way of your success. To the extent you can, evaluate the professional's advice. And recognize that even good investment programs go through rough patches.

Advice on Finding an Adviser

If you're looking for an adviser, consider the following observations and resources culled from Vanguard's long experience with clients and the industry.

- **What are your financial goals?** Are you looking for a comprehensive financial plan that includes investment management, tax planning, insurance planning, and estate planning? Some firms offer this broad array of financial planning services. Others focus on narrow areas, such as investment selection or retirement planning.
- **What do you expect from an adviser?** Do you want to handle some parts of your finances yourself or turn the whole thing over to a planner? Do you need a one-time consultation or ongoing monitoring and advice?
- **What are the adviser's experience and credentials?** An adviser can't be much help if he or she doesn't have experience with the services you need. Some advisers have professional credentials—CFP, CPA, PFS, CFA, ChFC*—that generally require a combination of work experience, formal study (including passing qualifying exams), and ongoing education. At the very least, these designations suggest a commitment to the field.
- **How is the adviser compensated?** A reputable adviser will be completely open and forthright when discussing compensation. Generally speaking, advisers are compensated through either commissions or fees. Commission-only advisers earn their income by selling financial products. The more the adviser sells and the greater the commission on a product, the more he or she earns, an arrangement that can be fraught with conflicts of interest.

  Fee-only advisers earn their income through fees based, for example, on an hourly rate, a flat annual or single-project amount, or an annual percentage of assets. A fee-only arrangement is generally preferable to a commission-based adviser, because a fee-only adviser's recommendations aren't influenced by compensation arrangements. Also, in a fee-only relationship, the costs of advice are crystal clear, which is not always the case in commission-based arrangements.
- **Are you comfortable with the adviser's professional and personal style?** If you plan to work with an adviser, you'll need to be honest

*Certified Financial Planner (CFP), Certified Public Accountant (CPA), Personal Financial Specialist (PFS), Chartered Financial Analyst (CFA), Chartered Financial Consultant (ChFC).

about your situation and goals. That can be difficult if you don't feel comfortable with the adviser. Interview several candidates to determine whether you feel comfortable with one.

- **What is the adviser's professional history?** You can do a background check on an adviser's credentials by contacting the professional organization that awards the designation. Check for any complaints or disciplinary actions with the National Association of Securities Dealers Regulation (telephone: 1-800-289-9999; online: www.nasdr.com) for registered representatives; the U.S. Securities and Exchange Commission (1-202-942-8090) for advisers who manage $25 million or more; or your state's securities commission (for advisers who manage less than $25 million). If the adviser is a registered investment adviser, ask for Form ADV (Parts I and II), which includes a variety of background information. The forms are also available online at www.adviserinfo.sec.gov.
- **Where to start?** If you don't know where to start looking for a planner, try the industry's various professional organizations (Table 3.5). Many mutual fund firms also offer various planning services to complement their investment management offerings.

TABLE 3.5 Organizations to Contact When Seeking an Adviser

Organization	*Contact for information on . . .*	*Phone number and Web address*
American Institute of Certified Public Accountants	CPAs who hold the Personal Financial Specialist (PFS) designation	1-888-999-9256 www.cpapfs.org
Financial Planning Association	Certified Financial Planners (CFPs)	1-800-322-4237 www.fpanet.org
National Association of Personal Financial Advisers	Fee-only financial planners	1-800-366-2732 www.napfa.org
Society of Financial Service Professionals	Advisers with at least one of any number of financial service credentials	1-888-243-2258 www.financialpro.org

Working on Your Own

If you plan to manage your own investments, our survey respondents noted that you're living in the best—and the worst—of times. You enjoy an unprecedented wealth of educational and informational resources, so much, in fact, that it's easy to become overwhelmed. Here are some experiences of do-it-yourselfers.

> "We were 40 when we began investing. Our six children began [investing] in their early 20s. There was little material for investor education when we began. Our children have the advantage of Morningstar [an investment research provider], newsletters, investment clubs, newspaper financial sections, etc."

> "In the mid-1960s, there weren't a whole lot of ways to educate yourself. There weren't these radio programs and television stations. Not a whole lot in the way of books."

> "There is actually too much advice. I am a physician and the same difficult situation exists [in my profession]. Novices can't really diagnose and treat their own problems. In a sense, the analogy holds. In medicine, the high ethical standards give people more trust in finding a doctor to help. I think that lack of trust in the investment industry leads to avoidance of the industry. That was true for me."

Our respondents shared some positive experiences about seeking the advice of family members and friends, as well as many stories about tips gone bad. Friends and family seemed to be most helpful in providing education about the broad principles of saving and investing. Another general finding: The closer the relationship, the more satisfactory the investment advice—a variation on the notion that "nobody cares as much about your money as you do." Your spouse is one degree removed from your financial fortunes. Your friends have less at stake.

> "My husband read a great deal, both for his work and for our benefit. He would listen to the financial programs on television. For myself, he would tell me things—he was ill for three years before he died—he was very keen on teaching me what he could before he died. So he tried to explain, advise, give me general tips about what I should do."

> "I have always been too conservative to get in much trouble, but once, upon the recommendation of a friend of mine in the insurance business, I bought USF&G and held it as the only stock in my IRA. It had a dividend yield at the time of 12%. I figured I could not beat that buying growth stocks, and thought USF&G was solid. It wasn't. I lost $22,000 pretty quick, and it hurt. I am not a rich man."

Advice from Market Veterans

Most of the investors surveyed choose to make their own investment decisions, a preference that reflects some combination of Vanguard's roots serving self-directed investors, confidence in their own ability to manage their portfolios, and at least some interest in investing.

About one-fourth of these investors worked with an adviser. If you decide on that course, you'll need to invest some time in finding a good one. Once you've retained a professional, however, the educational demands are less. The do-it-yourself investor will need to spend more time on the basics and on developing a plan to meet his or her goals. Your learning will most likely include a combination of reading, study, and real-world lessons in the markets. The "What Works" investors have words of wisdom for both groups, though clearly they don't speak with one voice.

> "Invest regularly after developing a financial plan. Do your own research if you have the time and ability; if not, seek impartial

professional advice (not at all easy to find). The main thing: Stick to the plan."

"People with limited capital will be better served allowing someone else to make their decisions."

"Get professional advice early. Keep it simple."

"Brokers put their pants on one leg at a time, like everyone else, and notwithstanding their familiarity with terms, buzzwords, etc. They are no more reliable at predicting security performance than the client. So I listen, but I make my own decisions. The results may not always be 'chic,' but I'm not being steamrolled."

"Everyone makes mistakes, and everyone does some things right. Learn from the mistakes. In any job, the first year is 'learning where all the bathrooms are.' After that come the nuances of the job, experience. Add to that a bit of luck, good market years, good judgment, wisdom in life's choice, and all will be well."

"It takes years of careful trial-and-error experience. You can't learn to swim on dry land, and you can't learn investing out of a book. Investing money is hard work, and you only learn by doing it."

"Our first investment in mutual funds was 1970. Six months later it had lost half the value. Then came the '73–'74 market. It was 1982 before things improved. Luckily we were too busy with family responsibilities to get hysterical about it. We use our experience to educate our children to play for the long haul. Make your mistakes. Educate yourself and hang in there."

"There are a great many well-written books that attempt to explain how the economy works. Read them, then start investing."

"If you learn from your investment experiences, it's all successful."

And if you can learn from someone else's mistakes, there's a chance you can avoid making them.

Education and the Cost of Ignorance

by Michael S. Miller

Michael S. Miller is managing director and head of Vanguard's Planning and Development group, whose functions include investor communications and public relations, portfolio review, corporate strategic planning, and investment counseling and research. Mr. Miller joined Vanguard in 1996.

Chances are you've seen the bumper sticker proclaiming, "If you think education is expensive, try ignorance." This thought is especially true for investing, where major mistakes can be very costly.

The good news is that learning about investing isn't necessarily expensive or all that complicated. The keys to successful investing are all pretty basic concepts. You have to live beneath your means so that you're regularly socking some money away in your investments. You want to control risk by having a diversified portfolio of funds (or of many individual securities), including a balanced mix of stock and bond funds (or individual securities). You want to keep costs low, so that your money is working hardest for *you*, not for a salesperson or investment firm. And you want to allow your investment plan to work over time, so that the power of compounding does its magic.

As investors in *Wealth of Experience* have made clear, you can learn the basics of investing by doing some independent reading and talking to family or friends whose experiences you value. Experience is a great teacher, too, as you've heard from the "What Works" respondents. But to minimize the tuition you pay to the school of hard knocks, don't take risks with a big portion of your money until you've really done your homework. Even if you decide to have a professional manage your money, I strongly recommend that you heed the advice of several investors in this chapter: Study things enough so that you understand what the adviser is doing. As a couple of your fellow investors said, "No one cares as much about your money as you do."

Many investors choose professionals to do at least some of the work of accumulating and managing wealth, whether it's managing a mutual fund or drawing up a financial plan. This is akin to relying on a physician because you value the professional training and experience the doctor has acquired. Yet we can be better patients for our doctors, and help ourselves in the process, by knowing enough to ask good questions, by monitoring our health, and by following the prescribed regimens.

Fortunately, most aspects of investing are far simpler than brain surgery. Yet plenty of people in the financial business have a vested interest in making the subject seem quite complex, or in making you feel that you may be missing out by not investing in the latest hot product.

Acquiring Knowledge a Sip at a Time

These days, investing information and opinions spew forth like water from a fire hose. Prices change every few seconds, and news about companies and the economy is issued nearly every hour of every day, in print, over the airwaves, and on the Internet. But there's no need to try to drink from the fire hose. Exposure to this daily flood of information is not crucial to being a successful investor. In fact, numerous studies have shown that reacting to all these developments and opinions by trading frequently is apt to be quite harmful to your financial health.

Instead of trying to keep on top of everything—a hopeless task no matter how much time you spend—try spending a little time reading up on the basics of investing. As little as 30 minutes a day, applied regularly over a few months, would be plenty of time to soak up key investing concepts and lessons. If you're highly motivated and want to spend more time, that's great. But there's no need to be in a rush. If you're unsure about an investment decision, keep the money in a bank account or money market fund while you do your homework and think things through.

Where to Start? Some Reading Recommendations

As you continue your investing education, you'll find sources that you consider helpful and trustworthy. I'll offer some recommendations here, erring on the side of brevity at the risk of leaving off the list some very fine Web sites, writers, and publications. Still, the truth is that the list of true investment classics—books that are likely to be worth reading for years to come—is not a long one.

You need not spend a fortune to educate yourself. A number of Web sites provide good data for free, and most local libraries carry the main financial magazines and the best of the investment books. Your local newspaper may be a good source for information. Financial journalists have grown in number and sophistication over the years, and the best of them are very much worth reading. As an investor, I've learned a lot from journalists who focus on the fundamentals of investing and financial planning rather than on individual products or services—writers such as Jason Zweig of *Money* magazine; Jonathan Clements of the *Wall Street Journal*; Jane Bryant Quinn of *Newsweek* magazine; and syndicated newspaper columnists Scott Burns, Russ Wiles, and Humberto Cruz.

As noted, there are many commercial Web sites operated by investment analysts and investment companies. I'll mention just one noncommercial site as a solid starting point: the Securities and Exchange Commission's Online Publications (www.sec.gov/investor/pubs.shtml).

When it comes to books, I hope you'll find this one helpful, of course. The following brief list, arranged alphabetically by author, includes other basic investment guides as well as some more advanced fare.

Against the Gods: The Remarkable Story of Risk, by Peter L. Bernstein.

Common Sense on Mutual Funds: New Imperatives for the Intelligent Investor, by John C. Bogle.

Straight Talk on Investing: What You Need to Know, by Jack Brennan with Marta McCave.

Winning the Loser's Game, by Charles D. Ellis.

A Random Walk Down Wall Street, by Burton G. Malkiel.

Making the Most of Your Money, by Jane Bryant Quinn.

The Only Investment Guide You'll Ever Need: How to Manage Your Money in Today's Economy, by Andrew Tobias.

chapter four

DIVERSIFY YOUR ASSETS

As "What Works" investors graduated from saving to investing, they began to use new tools: stocks, bonds, and money market instruments. Some purchased alternative investments such as limited partnerships and real estate. In the process, they faced the universal investment challenge of allocating their assets so as to balance the need—or desire—to earn high returns with their capacity to assume risk.

In this chapter, survey respondents relate lessons learned from their tentative first steps out of savings and into investments. Over the past 20 years, Americans have experienced a revolution in personal finance. In 1999, 80 million Americans—about half of U.S. households—participated in the stock market. In 1980, the number of stock market investors was 30 million, representing about 22% of U.S. households.[1]

The "What Works" investors have been foot soldiers in this campaign. Their experiences illustrate that an understanding of basic investment tools and concepts, including diversification and asset allocation, is key to the successful implementation of a personal investment plan.

Stocks, Bonds, and Cash: Risks and Rewards

"Do your homework. Buy blue chips and hang on. Diversification among stocks, bonds, and cash is important." The investors offered several variations on the advice of this 81-year-old retiree from New Jersey. Stocks, bonds, and cash—the three primary asset classes—each play a distinct role in your portfolio.

Primary Asset Classes Defined

- **Cash investments**, also known as *money market instruments, cash reserves*, or simply *cash*, are short-term (usually less than 90 days) IOUs issued by governments, corporations, banks, or other financial institutions.
- **Bonds** are also IOUs, or debt, issued by corporations or governments. An investor lends the bond issuer money for a specified period of time. In exchange, the bond issuer promises to repay the money at a specified date in the future and to make periodic interest payments in the interim. Usually, the amount of interest paid—the coupon—is fixed at a set percentage of the amount invested, which is why bonds are called fixed income investments. Over time, this interest income accounts for most of a bond's total return. Bonds with longer maturities generally offer a higher level of interest, or yield, but their prices are less stable. Shorter-term bonds provide greater stability, but generally less income.
- **Stocks**, also known as *equities*, represent part ownership in corporations. If an investor purchases one share in McDonald's, for example, that investor becomes a 0.00000008% owner of the fast-food giant.[2] Some corporations pay out part of their profits to stockholders in the form of dividends, though most corporations reinvest some or all of their profits in their businesses.

Table 4.1 shows that over time, stocks have provided the highest returns of the three major asset classes: 10.69% a year, on average, since 1926 through 2001. But that simple average conceals some wild ups and downs. About two-thirds of the stock market's yearly returns have fallen between –9.36% and 30.74%. In its worst year, 1931, the U.S. stock

TABLE 4.1 Returns and Risks of the Major Asset Classes: 1926–2001

	Average annual return (%)	*Typical annual range* (%)*	*Worst loss (%) (year)*
Stocks	10.69	–9.36 to 30.74	–43.13 (1931)
Bonds	5.67	–3.05 to 14.39	–8.11 (1969)
Cash	3.95	0.75 to 7.15	0.00 (1939 & 1940)

Source: The Vanguard Group, Inc.

*Defined as one standard deviation from average return. Standard deviation of stocks = 20.05; of bonds = 8.72; of cash = 3.2.

market lost 43.13% of its value. The main reason to invest in stocks is to pursue the high rates of long-term return necessary to achieve significant long-term goals.

From 1926 through 2001, bonds have provided average annual returns of 5.67%, with a typical range of –3.05% to 14.39%. In its worst year, the broad U.S. bond market returned –8.11%. Bonds have thus provided lower long-term returns than stocks, but with less dramatic ups and downs. Investors typically purchase bonds to generate income and moderate the risk of a stock-heavy portfolio.

Cash investments, as represented by U.S. Treasury bills, have returned an average of 3.95% a year since 1926. The typical variation from this average return has been 3.2 percentage points, up or down. In their worst years (1939 and 1940), T-bills produced 0% returns. Cash reserves can serve as a safe, liquid source of funds for short-term needs and emergencies, but their long-term returns have barely kept pace with the rising cost of living. If prices go up by 4% a year and you earn 3%, your money is losing purchasing power.

In general, stocks and bonds are *investment* assets used to meet long-term financial goals. Cash is a *savings* assets used to earn safe, but modest, returns on money that you'll need relatively soon—within one to two years, for example.

Diversify, Diversify!

The asset-class statistics just presented represent the performance of broad stock and bond market indexes, or benchmarks. These results are analogous to the returns—and the risks—you probably would have experienced in broadly *diversified* portfolios of stocks and bonds (though the real-world costs of investing would have reduced real-world returns). These returns have no relation to the returns an investor would have experienced in any particular stock, bond, or cash instrument, which *could* have been higher or lower, and *would* have been riskier.

Diversification means spreading your money among different classes of financial assets and among the securities of many issuers, and it is an essential strategy in investing. Diversifying your investments helps to smooth out the ups and downs in your portfolio. By combining different assets that produce different patterns of return, you reduce a portfolio's volatility without a commensurate sacrifice in potential return. That's why diversification has been called a free lunch.

Indexes: The Market's Measuring Sticks

Many of the investors mentioned indexes and the index funds that attempt to match the performance of these benchmarks. An index is a gauge that measures the performance of the stock market or bond market or subsectors of either one. The first (and still most widely recognized) index was the Dow Jones Industrial Average, created by Charles Dow in 1896 to track the performance of the U.S. stock market. Other major indexes are listed below.

Stocks

- **Wilshire 5000 Total Market Index**. The broadest measure of the U.S. stock market, this index tracks the stocks of virtually every publicly traded company.
- **Wilshire 4500 Completion Index**. Tracks the portion of the U.S. stock market not included in the Standard & Poor's 500 Index.
- **Standard & Poor's 500 Index**. Tracks 500, mostly large-capitalization, stocks representing more than 75% of the value of all U.S. stocks.

- **Nasdaq Composite Index**. Tracks more than 5,000 stocks traded on the Nasdaq Stock Exchange; during the 1990s, it became a widely watched barometer for technology stocks.
- **Russell 1000 Index**. Tracks the 1,000 largest U.S. stocks.
- **Russell 2000 Index**. Tracks 2,000 small-capitalization stocks.
- **Morgan Stanley Capital International Europe, Australasia, Far East (MSCI EAFE) Index**. Tracks the world's major non-U.S. stock markets.
- **MSCI Europe Index**. EAFE subindex that tracks European stocks.
- **MSCI Pacific Index**. EAFE subindex that tracks Pacific Rim stocks.

Bonds

- **Lehman Brothers Government Bond Index**. Tracks U.S. government agency and Treasury bonds.
- **Lehman Corporate Bond Index**. Tracks fixed-rate, nonconvertible, investment-grade corporate bonds.
- **Lehman Mortgage-Backed Securities Index**. Tracks fixed-rate securities of the Government National Mortgage Association (GNMA), the Federal National Mortgage Association (FNMA), and the Federal National Loan Mortgage Corporation (FNLMC).
- **Lehman Aggregate Bond Index**. The broadest measure of the taxable U.S. bond market, tracking most Treasury, agency, corporate, mortgage-backed, asset-backed, and international dollar-denominated issues.
- **Lehman High Yield Index**. Tracks corporate bonds with credit ratings that are below investment-grade.
- **Lehman Municipal Bond Index**. Tracks investment-grade tax-exempt bonds that are issued by state and local governments.

In the stock market, diversification means investing in many stocks of different-sized companies with varying market capitalizations and investment characteristics (that is, small-cap, mid-cap, or large-cap, and fast- or slower-growing companies) from different industries. If you invest in bonds, diversification means holding securities from many different issuers (though if you invest in U.S. Treasury bonds, diversification isn't essential—the U.S. government isn't going to go out of business).

"All of your investments should not be going up at the same time," noted one investor. Or down, we might add. The more widely you diversify, the more likely it is that a period of positive returns from, say, health care stocks will offset a weak spell in technology stocks, or that strong results from bonds will limit the damage from a sharp decline in stock prices. Although diversification offers no defense against market risk—the possibility of a generalized decline in securities prices—it reduces the risk that the performance of any one security will torpedo your portfolio, a lesson learned the hard way by several investors.

> "Silly me. I got caught up in the euphoria and I invested in highly risky tech funds. I am lucky I didn't throw a lot of money in this direction, but enough that it hurt, and I got burned."

> "I made and lost a lot of money while investing in high-tech stocks and growth mutual funds. I have learned a lot since the recent decline. Diversification will be a higher priority in the future."

A Boston-area investor who said he'd take above-average risks for above-average gains nevertheless advocated the time-tested and conservative principle of diversification. He noted that a common mistake among investors was "betting too heavily on any one stock or sector. One out of 10 times you'll be a hero—9 out of 10, a goat."

> "In July of 2000, I sold half of my Microsoft stock and then turned around and bought more tech stocks, thinking I was diversifying and not putting all my money on one stock. Needless to say, I have lost almost all the money I invested in tech stocks. I wish I had not sold my Microsoft stock."

> "Many investors gamble on one or a few stocks and do not keep a percentage of their assets in cash or bonds. Many investors

purchase the stock of the company that they work for. They believe in their employer's successful management of the company and invest too heavily in its stock (as I did)."

Several investors commented on the heightened risks of investing heavily in their employers' stock. Employees may receive attractive incentives to invest, such as a discount on the stock's market price, but too much of a good thing can be dangerous. "Very early on, I put all of my eggs in one basket. When my employers went to hell, I lost both my job and my savings," said one.

Another investor who works in an industry that has experienced waves of layoffs in recent years put the risks of investing heavily in his company's stock in terms of a broad portfolio including not only your investments but also the income you earn from working:

"I'll tell you one insight someone once told me that goes to this whole idea of people putting everything in one stock, or their company stock. Think of your job as a bond and the income you get from your job as the interest on your bond. So if you earn $100,000 a year, and interest rates are 5%, you've got the equivalent of a $2 million bond in your company [$100,000 salary/5% interest rate = $2 million]. So you've already got a huge investment in your job. Do you really want to invest any more in your company?"

Alternative Investments

The experiences of "What Works" investors overall suggest that there's no need to venture beyond simple, liquid stocks, bonds, and cash. But some have. They've invested in real estate, gold and silver, and limited partnerships (most of which were destroyed by tax reforms in 1986) that pursued a variety of objectives (avocado farming, for one), most with the goal of minimizing the partners' income taxes.

Just as in the liquid financial markets, the survey respondents have enjoyed successes and disappointments with alternative investments. One big difference is that these investments may demand expertise in a highly specialized area: timber harvesting in the case of one investor, sod farming in the case of another. Their risks can be hard to evaluate, too, and if your goals change, or your investment goes bad, assets such as real estate and limited partnerships can be difficult to exit. Although alternative investments no doubt enhance a portfolio's diversification, they also add to its complexity, cost, and time demands.

> "Fifteen years ago, my husband and I invested in a real estate limited partnership, recommended by a highly respected financial adviser. We were wary of this investment, but agreed to look into it. Several weeks later, after doing our homework, we decided it was not for us, and opted to withdraw from the proposed partnership. Although nothing had been signed, the financial adviser said, 'You can't do that!' I think that legally, we could have withdrawn, but we very reluctantly went through with the investment and subsequently lost nearly all of the $100,000 involved."

> "I invested in a real estate limited partnership on my broker's advice. It went totally down the tubes."

> "When I first began to invest outside of pension plans, I read an article that said a certain percentage of one's assets should be in gold as an inflation hedge. I put a few thousand dollars in a gold fund, which dropped 25% before I received my confirmation slip. Lessons: Don't believe a lot of what you read, and don't put a lot of money in narrow sectors that you don't understand."

> "I was convinced to buy land in Florida, an undeveloped building lot. I was told it would appreciate rapidly. I learned that associated annual fees (maintenance, taxes, membership, etc.)

were an unexpected burden and eroded any appreciation. I also learned that we couldn't easily sell the lot. It took a long time to get the money back. Lessons: Beware the cost of investing and be sure to understand the market for your investment."

When these alternative investments perform well, however, the rewards can be especially sweet. Assets such as real estate, or even a privately owned business, can provide tangible satisfactions that you just can't get from a portfolio of stocks, bonds, and cash. These assets may also satisfy investment—and noninvestment—objectives. Real estate can generate financial returns, but it's also a place to live. Business owners can earn returns on their ownership in an enterprise above and beyond a salary paid by the same enterprise.

"I bought part of a professional practice, then bought the rest. I added associates and built a new clinic. Between selling corporate shares (built up with sweat equity) and renting the clinic to the practice, I have sold shares I paid nothing for and have a way to get money out of the corporation by high rents that flow to me."

"My major investment has been land. I bought 80 acres of land north of Spokane, Washington. Over 25 years, I've been able to log the 80 acres three times with selective cutting."

"Our most successful investment was the purchase of our second house, which we planned and built. We worked with a respected architect and a well-established, reputable builder, and chose an upscale community with good schools, in a convenient Boston suburb. We kept an eagle eye on every step of the building process. We loved that house and lived in it happily for 24 years, and when we sold it when my husband retired, its value had increased tenfold. Lessons: Do your research, look for high quality at a fair price, and pay attention to your investment during the time you own it."

> "We purchased a New Jersey shore home that we enjoyed for five seasons. Rented for two weeks each summer (IRS allows tax-free), covering much of the expenses. It doubled in price, and we sold it last fall! I believe this is the next bubble to burst. Regardless, we had fun and made sizable profit."

> "Our most successful investment experiences were in real estate located in the Washington, D.C., area in the 1970s and '80s. I guess the lesson I learned was that, when the government is willing to subsidize certain economic activities, as they did for real estate (through income tax deductions and low interest rates), one should take advantage of it, and profit from it, provided that you don't overpay and don't overleverage."

Among the respondents, real estate was the most popular complement to stocks, bonds, and cash, but it's not for everyone. You may have to become a landlord and building manager, or hire someone else to do it. If the investment pays off, however, it can provide an additional level of portfolio diversification as well as attractive returns, as one woman told us.

> "We were 27 and 28 years old. We did not want a house yet because we wanted to do some traveling. Between the two of us we had about $5,000. I remember taking a class at UCLA in property management. And I remember them saying that you wanted to buy a building that's within walking distance of shopping, close to public transportation. I told a broker this is what we were looking for, and I believe we looked at one building. It was $55,000, and it was $5,000 down. Now it's to the point where it's making a lot of money for us. It replaces half of a professional salary. We only pay $800 a month for the mortgage, and it brings in $52,000 a year. In retirement, if you add that income to two double-income maximum Social Security payments, it's tremendous. It has been a really good investment."

This woman said that she and her husband "are probably one of the few couples that have not been hurt by everything that has been going on" in the tough stock markets of 2000, 2001, and 2002.

What about the hassles of maintenance, managing the building? "When they see me, an older woman, sweeping the driveway once a week, they're less likely to put crud on the sidewalks. Tenants consider it their home." Still, "sometimes it can be very scary. I had a drug dealer who moved into the building once, and someone shot into the building. I don't want you to think it's a bad neighborhood, but it's Los Angeles, and sometimes people pull the wool over your eyes."

Asset Allocation

Just as these investors cautioned us to diversify *within* an asset class, they counseled us to do the same thing *among* the various asset classes by investing in stocks, bonds, and cash, and—if you are so inclined—alternative investments such as real estate.

How you divide your assets among stocks, bonds, and cash is the main factor in both your portfolio's long-term returns and the fluctuations in its value. An all-stock portfolio has historically provided the highest returns, but with bone-rattling fluctuations in value. A cash portfolio has experienced much less dramatic ups and downs, but the long-term returns have been modest. Table 4.2 displays four sample allocations of stocks and bonds labeled according to their risk-return profiles: growth, moderate growth, conservative growth, and income.

The key to your own asset allocation is your investment plan. As discussed in Chapter 2, your plan takes into account the amount of time you have to reach your goal and the level of returns you'll need to get there. Both factors help you determine an appropriate asset allocation. You'll also need to consider your appetite for risk. There's probably no avoiding risk. Building the wealth to pay for ambitious goals such as retirement generally requires some exposure to higher-risk, potentially higher-returning, assets such as stocks. But if you stretch too far beyond

TABLE 4.2 Returns and Risks of Sample Asset Allocations: 1926–2001

	Average annual return (%)	*Worst annual loss (%) (year)*	*Number of years with a loss*
Growth (80% stocks/20% bonds)	10.0	–34.9 (1931)	21 of 76
Moderate growth (60% stocks/40% bonds)	9.1	–26.6 (1931)	19 of 76
Conservative growth (40% stocks/60% bonds)	8.1	–18.4 (1931)	16 of 76
Income (20% stocks/80% bonds)	7.0	–10.1 (1931)	13 of 76

Source: The Vanguard Group, Inc.

your comfort level, you may be unable to stick with your plan. "Unsuccessful investors are thrilled when investments go up and depressed or terrified when the market goes down," one woman noted. "They panic, of course, and buy on the high side and sell on the down. I think they do this because they don't know their risk tolerance, and they don't have short-, medium-, and long-term investments that are matched to their goals."

Discovering your own risk tolerance may take time. Some investors didn't understand their true appetites for risk until they were in the middle of a tough situation. Others ventured into the financial markets and then concluded that they hadn't taken enough risk, forfeiting the opportunity to earn higher long-term returns. Vanguard Chairman Jack Brennan has often noted that, for all the sophisticated asset-allocation tools and guides available, the simplest—and best—means of determining an appropriate mix is the *gut test*: If you're a nervous wreck, you've probably taken too much risk. But if your portfolio has no exposure to volatile assets, you probably haven't taken enough. The wisdom of this approach is clear in the responses of some investors.

"When I moved many of my funds for consolidation, I had a financial analysis performed by the recipient of my money. They advised repositioning my portfolio. I took most of the advice. I believe that had I retained my positions, I would have not been as vulnerable to market swings, both up and down. I am more risk-averse now and hope to reduce risk when the market recovers. Take advice carefully, assess your needs, and feel comfortable with your decisions."

"When I was working, I was 100% in equities and living out of current earnings; when I semi-retired I lowered my risk profile, but now query whether I stayed too aggressive. I am 60% in equities, consistent with what many experts say, but it hasn't felt that good lately."

"My biggest challenge was the bear market in 1973 and 1974. That was the biggest drop until that point. Up until then, everything had gone up. I persisted and dollar-cost averaged at that point. I was investing something like $150 per month during that period. Most of my investments had taken place before the big decline, so I didn't get the full benefit of the dollar-cost averaging, but I just hung in there until it came back."

"I was too conservative. I had too much emphasis on bonds, and my money grew too slowly. I should have been more aggressive concerning equity investments earlier in life."

"My most successful experience was switching from an asset allocation of one-half GICs [guaranteed investment contracts, conservative vehicles that pay a fixed rate of interest over a fixed period of time] and one-half equity funds to 100% equities in my early years of investing. Learned that you have to take risk to make money."

Once you've discovered how much risk you're willing to bear, you can develop, or fine-tune, an asset allocation to meet the goals articulated in your investment plan.

The 'What Works' Allocations

Table 4.3 shows the average asset allocations of the "What Works" investors, grouped by age. These portfolios may not be appropriate to your own unique circumstances, but they illustrate general principles that are useful in allocating your assets. While stocks made up almost 55% of the portfolios of investors below age 60, the allocation to stocks decreased with advancing age. It's possible that older investors have met many of their goals and can afford to place less emphasis on stocks, the primary engines for long-term growth. Also, as investors age, their time horizons shorten, meaning that they have less time to recover from the stock market's periodic downturns.

The investors' average allocation to bonds was about 22% for those under age 60, a percentage that rose to nearly 30% for those aged 70 or older. Bonds can generate income for living expenses when you're no longer drawing a paycheck. In addition, the principal value of bonds is

TABLE 4.3 'What Works' Investors' Asset Allocations, by Age

	Under age 60 (%)	*Ages 60 to 69 (%)*	*Ages 70 or older (%)*
U.S. stocks	54.4	49.4	46.4
International stocks	4.0	4.0	2.0
Bonds	21.6	27.6	29.6
Money market funds	15.0	15.0	15.0
Other	5.0	4.0	7.0
Total	100.0	100.0	100.0

Source: The Vanguard Group, Inc.

more stable than that of stocks, so there's less risk of loss to investors with limited time and opportunity to recover.

The similarities in the investors' portfolios were just as instructive as the differences. All portfolios included significant allocations to both stocks and bonds. Consider that today's 70-year-olds may live another 30 years (or longer!). They will need some exposure to stocks to generate the asset growth necessary to keep pace with the rising cost of living. By the same token, a younger investor can benefit from exposure to lower-risk assets, such as bonds and money market funds. These assets moderate the ups and downs of a stock-heavy portfolio, which can give you the emotional fortitude to stick with a long-term program. They also protect against the unexpected. What if stocks don't provide higher returns than bonds during your investment time horizon? You're covered just in case.

Setting Your Own Allocation

Asset allocation is fundamentally about balancing your need, or desire, for gain with your capacity to assume risk. Only you can select the mix of stocks, bonds, and cash best suited to your needs and temperament, but our investors offered plenty of tips and food for thought.

> "Proceed cautiously. Go with a diversified U.S. fund. Branch out as you learn, read, and become more experienced. Don't get caught up in hype. Remember: It's your money, and when it's gone, it's gone. Preserve it. Your active verb should be 'save,' not 'invest.' "

> "Take your time, and research before investing. Don't take unnecessary risks that you cannot afford. Once you make your investment decisions, stay with them and be patient. Don't set unrealistic expectations. Look at investments for the long term. There really aren't any 'get-rich-quick' investments without huge risks."

The successful investor has "an ability to counter one's natural tendencies somewhat; if you are risk-averse/pessimistic, take on a little more risk than you feel comfortable with; if you are a risk-taker/optimistic, moderate your risk-taking a bit."

"Put your money in a balanced mutual fund. New investors hate losses. A balanced fund protects an investor from a major downturn. On the other hand, it will not grow as much as aggressive growth funds, but the increase is better than a savings account."

"Buy Vanguard 500 Index Fund or Total Stock Market Index Fund with 70% of your money and put 30% in 1-year Treasury bills."

"Buy an S&P 500 Index fund for stocks with 35% of your assets. Buy individual tax-free bonds with 60% of your assets if you have more than $500,000 in net worth. Put 5% in cash."

"Invest funds on a monthly basis in Vanguard 500 Index Fund (60%) and a short-term bond fund (40%). Maintain this routine while studying everything you can about investing. When you're ready, invest in carefully selected individual stocks."

"Spend less than you earn and invest the rest: 50% stock index fund, 50% bond index fund."

"Start now. Be consistent. Give up a few luxuries. Diversify. Don't forget bonds and real estate."

"Stick to bonds and funds when you build a nest egg. Never risk more than 35% in stocks. Wait until you have the money."

"1. Make an investment plan and stick to it. 2. Commit 100% minus your age to equities. 3. Use index funds for equities, especially S&P 500 Index. 4. Rebalance every 3 to 12 months. 5. Invest half of bonds in TIPs [Treasury inflation-protected securities] and half in Vanguard Total Bond Market Index Fund."

Your asset allocation is the big picture. In the next chapter, the investors shed light on the nitty-gritty details. Individual securities or funds? Managed funds or indexed funds? They discuss the pros and cons of different vehicles you can use to establish an allocation that will help you meet the goals laid out in your plan.

The Asset Allocation Constants

by Catherine D. Gordon

Catherine D. Gordon, principal, heads Vanguard's Investment Counseling & Research group, which sets investment policy and methodology used by Vanguard's advisory services and analyzes the investment issues faced by Vanguard's broad range of clients, from individual investors to large institutions. Ms. Gordon joined Vanguard in 1994.

Your asset allocation—the mix of stocks, bonds, cash, and any other assets you own—is ultimately the main determinant of your portfolio's returns. But the striking fact is that people often neglect this big-picture issue. They focus instead on selecting individual funds or stocks, wondering which will do best and worrying about those that have not performed well lately. A major bonus of focusing on asset allocation first is that it simplifies the task of selecting which funds or stocks to own.

But first, I'd emphasize an obvious point that's implicit in the comments of survey respondents: Investing is for long-term financial goals; saving is for meeting short-term needs. Your allocation for savings is simple: cash—short-term vehicles such as money market funds, bank accounts, or U.S. Treasury bills to protect principal. The risk of short-term price declines is too significant in the bond and stock markets to hazard money needed for short-term goals.

Asset allocation really pertains to investment goals such as managing the assets you're accumulating for—or spending in—retirement.

Characteristics of a Sensible Plan

Your asset allocation should reflect your financial needs, risk tolerance, and time horizon. These are the factors described in your investment plan. Obviously, the factors are different for everyone. People with modest assets and 40 years until retirement will probably have asset allocations that are very different from those of a 65-year-old of substantial means. But most sensible asset mixes share a few common traits.

First, an asset allocation should be balanced. An aggressive allocation designed to help you meet long-term goals will be heavily tilted toward stocks, and a conservative mix will include more bonds and cash. But just about every investor's portfolio should have some exposure to at least two of the three major asset classes: stocks, bonds, and cash.

In the late 1990s, you may have felt foolish investing in anything but stocks. Stocks were returning more than 20% a year, and bonds and cash looked poky. But from March 2000 to October 2002, the stock market experienced one of the most severe declines in history. Bonds were one of the financial markets' lone bright spots. You never know what returns will be. Balance gives us some protection against this uncertainty, and over time, diversifying across assets that behave differently can reduce your portfolio's risk level.

Second, a portfolio should be broadly diversified, both *across* and *within* asset classes. You have to be very careful about overweighting a particular part of the stock or bond market. If your stock portfolio, for example, looks very different from the broad stock market, you're assuming additional risk that may, or may not, pay off. During the dot.com heyday, people asked us why we didn't recommend overweighting technology stocks, or why we had no technology-stock fund. The sector was red-hot. Some shareholders thought we'd missed the boat, but we didn't have to think twice about it. Our core belief, based on experience and research, is that these concentrated bets are not a compelling risk-reward proposition, something that became all too clear when the tech bubble burst.

On a related note, I've observed that many investors think they're diversified simply because they own more than one fund, or maybe because they've bought different funds from different fund companies. But if you invest in a Vanguard growth fund, and then purchase another growth fund from another fund company, you're not diversifying. You're doing on the fund level what the respondent who sold Microsoft and "diversified" into tech stocks did at the individual-stock level: You're buying another flavor of what you own already.

Third, you should periodically rebalance your portfolio to maintain your target allocations. It doesn't really matter whether you rebalance annually, semiannually, or quarterly, but by rebalancing periodically, you limit the risk of having too much exposure to any one industry or investment style. People who sold stock funds and reinvested in bond funds during the late 1990s to maintain their target allocations are probably feeling a lot happier today than people who simply let their high-flying stocks ride—that ride was way up, then way down. And I'd guess that people who were rebalancing from bonds to stocks from March 2000 to October 2002 will be grateful for it down the road. The key is to be disciplined about rebalancing. Set a date to rebalance ahead of time rather than saying, "Well, first I'll see what the market does next week."

Your Own Allocation

Most investors can develop a reasonable allocation by observing these general principles and using a little common sense. You can't determine an allocation that's appropriate for you with absolute precision, such as 63.5% of your assets in U.S. stocks, 13.5% in international stocks, 17% in U.S. bonds, and 6% in cash. There is no right answer, but there are many reasonable answers.

I found it interesting that, as a group, the "What Works" investors had an asset mix that wasn't far off the classic allocation of 60% stocks and 40% bonds that has been used for decades by large institutional investors like endowment funds and foundations. This allocation isn't for everyone, but the challenge of an individual who is saving for a long-term goal like retirement isn't terribly different from the challenge of a pension fund or other institution that has to invest assets on behalf of many beneficiaries (except, of course, that an institution may have an indefinite time horizon, while ours are finite). In both cases, however, you need long-term growth as well as some balance to control the risk of market declines.

As you think about your own asset allocation, be sure to look over Table 4.1, which shows the range of returns for the major asset classes, and Table 4.2, which shows how various asset mixes have performed.

A person might logically ask, "Why not invest everything in stocks, since stocks historically have outpaced bonds and cash over the long term? We'd caution against a 100% allocation to stocks, even for an aggressive investor with a long time horizon, for two main reasons. First, there's no guarantee that stocks will always outperform bonds, even over long periods. History isn't certain to repeat. Second—and this is the more important reason—very few investors who hold only stocks have the fortitude to ride out a severe, prolonged market downturn (like the nearly 50% drop in U.S. stocks in 2000–2002). And you can't reap the long-term rewards of stocks if the pain gets too severe and you sell them after they've fallen.

On the other hand, it would be a mistake to pursue short-term safety at all costs. It may be tempting to avoid stocks because you don't think you can stomach the market's periodic downturns, but if you reduce your exposure to market risk, you may be increasing your exposure to *shortfall risk*—the risk that your assets won't grow enough to help you meet your future financial needs.

Secondary Considerations

One thing I found encouraging about these investors' asset allocations is that, on average, they have some exposure to international stocks. There's been debate in recent years about whether international stocks still provide any portfolio diversification. And a few years before the current debate, during the U.S. stock market's late-1990s run-up, people were arguing that U.S. investments would produce the highest returns, so there was no reason to invest abroad.

However, we've been saying for years that international funds may make sense for you if you're aiming to diversify your portfolio and you can withstand the additional risks. (In addition to all the regular stock market risks, there may be currency and political risks associated with international stocks. When international currencies rise or fall against the U.S. dollar, the value of international stocks falls or rises in dollar terms.) The degree of the diversification benefit from holding international stocks varies over time, but we believe the benefit continues to exist.

As a rule, however, most investors should limit their international stock holdings to no more than 20% of their overall stock position. This enables you to get the benefits of additional portfolio diversification without adding undue risk to your portfolio. The exact allocation, however, should be based on *your* financial goals, time horizon, and risk tolerance, not on a guideline or rule of thumb.

Several investors mentioned assets such as real estate, gold, or limited partnerships. These investments can provide additional diversification, but I'd say that you can get most of what you need from traditional liquid assets like stocks, bonds, and cash. When it comes to figuring out an allocation appropriate for your circumstances, these alternatives are not a big factor.

Action Steps

- Find a balanced mix of stocks, bonds, and cash that is appropriate to the unique goals and circumstances detailed in your investment plan. Don't confuse saving and investing.
- Diversify across and within asset classes. Overweighting a particular security or sector of the financial markets exposes you to risks that may or may not pay off.
- Rebalance periodically to your target allocation. Although the frequency isn't all that important, it's important to rebalance from time to time to keep your portfolio's risk and return characteristics in line with your goals.

chapter five
SELECT YOUR INVESTMENTS

There are two ways to invest in the financial markets: through individual securities or the mutual funds that hold them. Many "What Works" investors do both, as illustrated in Figure 5.1. On average, they keep

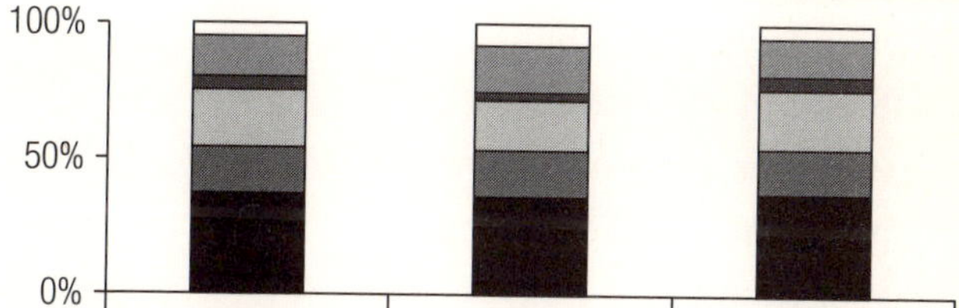

	Total (%)	Core (%)	High-net-worth (%)
☐ Other instruments	5	8	5
Money market funds	15	17	14
Individual bonds	5	3	5
Bond funds	22	18	22
Individual stocks	17	17	17
Stock funds	37	36	38

FIGURE 5.1 'What Works' investors' mix of funds and individual securities.

Source: The Vanguard Group, Inc.

Note: Columns don't add to 100% because of rounding.

17% of their total assets (and about one-third of their stock assets) in individual stocks. About 5% of their total assets (and 19% of their bond assets) are invested in individual securities.

In this chapter, "What Works" investors review the benefits and trade-offs of investing in funds and individual securities. The experiences of respondents in selecting investments have also led them to consider another issue: the ability of any investor, amateur or professional, to select investments that will outperform the broad market's returns over time. This question can't be answered definitively, but our investors had strong opinions.

Stock Mutual Funds Versus Individual Stocks

One of the great advantages of mutual funds is that they can provide instant diversification with the purchase of a single fund share. A broadly diversified stock fund holds hundreds or thousands of stocks from different-sized companies in different stages of growth and in different industries. By investing in just one diversified fund, you limit the damage that the blowup of any one security could do to your portfolio. (There are specialized funds, too, that focus on narrow sectors of the market, or even on single industries, but a mainstream growth or growth-and-income stock fund provides broad diversification.) Among these investors, the mutual fund proponents identified diversification as perhaps the most compelling reason to invest in funds rather than individual securities.

> "People make the mistake of buying individual stocks as opposed to funds. Look at great buys in the past—Xerox, AOL, WorldCom, now the banks, etc. The list goes on. Mutual funds give you diversity!"

> "Buy funds instead of individual stocks. You can't get stung as much."

"I jumped on some high-risk technology issues, such as Global Crossing near the 1999–2000 market peak, and rode them down. The experience has dampened my desire to do a lot of stock picking. I will mainly use mutual funds for the equity portion of my holdings, as the volatility of this market can kill you on individual stocks."

People stumble by "investing in an individual stock instead of an indexed mutual fund that provides broad diversification. People think they can make a strong, quick return because they've heard stories from others."

"I have invested in penny stocks. I was well aware of the risks involved. After losing $4,000, I found out that the last transaction was pure fraud. I have a certificate for 60,000 shares in a company that never existed. Some of the brokerage people went to prison for securities fraud. The lesson I learned was that businesspeople are not properly watched. I never invested in individual stocks or bonds again."

"My best experience has been investing totally in mutual funds (exclusive of muni bonds) and eventually moving to index funds almost exclusively. The only individual company shares I have owned during the last 15+ years were in companies on whose board I sat (including the public company of which I was CEO)."

Despite appreciating the diversification benefits of funds, many of the investors we surveyed are deeply involved in personally managing portfolios of individual stocks. In some cases, these holdings may be an accident of history. "When we first got involved, mutual funds weren't awfully well known," said a retired investor from Pennsylvania who began buying stocks in the early 1960s. "There were no company plans. You just worked, put in your time, and got a pension. There was nothing like 401(k)s, which encourage people to invest in the markets. I suspect that we were in the minority in our attitude toward investing."

Today, mutual funds are everywhere. At the end of 2001, there were more than 8,000 stock, bond, and money market funds, holding almost $7 trillion in assets.[1] Yet 30 or 40 years ago, mutual funds were barely a footnote in household balance sheets. In 1960, according to the U.S. Federal Reserve, mutual funds accounted for less than 2% of household assets.[2] "There was no such thing as investing," one man told us. "Investing was for rich people."

If people invested in stocks at all at that time, they most likely did so through directly held securities (constituting 36% of household assets in December 1960, including holdings in private and public companies) or life insurance policies with an investment component (8% of household assets in 1960).[3] "When we were first married, there were no so-called mutual fund companies," said one woman, describing her first investments 40 years ago. "The first investment I remember doing was my husband's life insurance policy." (The first mutual fund began operations in 1924, but her point is well taken: Mutual funds were a cottage industry until the 1970s.)

By 2000, mutual funds made up almost 14% of household assets. Individually owned stocks accounted for 25% of assets, and life insurance reserves for less than 3%.[4] But mutual funds' obscurity 40 years ago doesn't entirely explain the current popularity of individual stocks. "I read Malkiel [Princeton University economics professor and author of *A Random Walk Down Wall Street*] in my twenties," said one investor. "I've become an indexer, but one thing I liked about Malkiel is, he said that you should index, but if you want to have some fun, go ahead and buy individual stocks.[5] I have about 60% in individual stocks and funds—mostly index funds—for the rest." For some investors, stocks are simply more engaging, even entertaining, than funds. Stock picks dominated the discussion of the "What Works" respondents' best investments, as reflected below.

> "I bought 100 shares of Cisco, saw the investment increase in value sevenfold in four years, and then sold it. I made five times my initial investment."

"I bought Burr-Brown in 1993 for $7,000. After many splits, I cashed in $120,000 and have 800 shares of Texas Instruments. Buy quality and hold for the long term."

"When Philip Morris fell into the $20s, I started buying all the way down to $19. I accumulated enough shares to ensure me a dividend income of $54,000 per year. I was satisfied, but when it rose into the $50s, I sold and put $1.2 million into long-term bonds for an income of around $80,000 per year."

"I did well with Oshkosh Truck. Bought it when it was coming out of bankruptcy at $11 and sold at $59.81, after a 3 for 2 split and dividend. Bought Myriad Genetics stock at $8 and sold two months later at $124."

"My best experience was with IBM stock. I bought it at $80, as I remembered that it had once been at $150. It then went down to $45 and started upward again. At $50, I bought another lot, thinking that in 30 days I could sell my first lot for a tax deduction. However, it kept going up, and I never sold any at all. Over the years since 1987, it split to four times the number of shares and four times the investment."

Mutual funds may not deliver quick riches and action-packed excitement, but they generally don't sustain hair-raising declines, at least relative to individual stocks. As William J. Bernstein, author of *The Four Pillars of Investing: Lessons for Building a Winning Portfolio*, put it, "In investing, it's all too often true that the same things that maximize your chances of getting rich also maximize your chances of getting poor."[6] Investment research firm Morningstar calculated that during 2000–2001, more than 31% of all stocks lost at least half their value. During the same period, only 5.3% of stock mutual funds lost as much. Some of our investors reached similar conclusions in the real-world laboratories of their own portfolios.

"One stock constituted 15% of my net worth (Global Crossing). I rode it all the way down to Global Crossing's bankruptcy. Lesson: Diversify."

"In 1968, I purchased stock in a company I did legal work for; it was an IPO [initial public offering]. It failed. It was an expensive lesson to learn that you don't get rich quick and you don't buy individual stocks."

"I invested $2,000 in the IPO of an acquaintance whose company I believed was a great idea. It's now worth nothing (although it's still in my portfolio)."

"My most disappointing experience was buying Lucent. I believed Lucent was part of the telephone company. It was safe in my mind, a stock for widows and orphans. They were top class. I did feel funny buying a stock with such a low dividend. Then when it made big drops in one day, I didn't know things were going wrong. Due to lack of information and not knowing what they did, I set myself up for disaster."

Professional Management

Some "What Works" investors valued the professional investment expertise available through actively managed mutual funds (that is, funds whose managers assess the value of different securities in an attempt to beat the returns of the financial markets). Others were skeptical that such expertise exists at all. Those who conceded that it might exist doubted that the average investor is capable of identifying this superior ability in advance. After all, the securities markets are made up of hundreds of thousands of professionals, many with years of training, advanced degrees from the best schools, and enormous resources at their disposal, all competing against one another for a marginal advantage.

Even if an investor, amateur or professional, succeeds in identifying superior investments, the cost of doing so (in terms of time, research expenses, and transaction costs) may wipe out his or her incremental gains. The data from the mutual fund industry lend strong, if not conclusive, support to this line of reasoning.[7] Among the investors, those skeptical of investment talent invested in indexed mutual funds—portfolios that buy and hold the stocks or bonds, or a representative sample, of market indexes—seeking to match the returns of the market averages and minimizing the amount lost to investment costs. (Such an investment strategy is called *passive management*.) Both the indexers and the believers in investment talent made their cases forcefully.

The Active Advocates

> "Mutual funds offer the best opportunity to be ahead of the information curve if managed properly."

> "My best experience was moving from individual stocks to mutual funds. I learned I was right when I had concluded I couldn't pick when to buy, and especially when to sell, individual stocks—particularly in competition with professional, full-time experts."

> One investor noted his best investment experience was staying "with proven financial managers who share my values/philosophy. This means swallowing hard in times of underperformance."

> Another noted that his best decision was "placing all of my (our) assets into Vanguard, and investing in mutual funds. I would say that the Health Care Fund was our most successful investment. I learned that I should put my trust in mutual fund managers, since they have the resources to manage our assets correctly."

The Indexers

"I'm a big believer in indexing. 'Experts' who think they can consistently beat the market are just laughable. What a bunch of windbags they are. Just because they're on TV doesn't mean they know anything. I get sick of reading *Money* magazine. None of the articles mention how much those portfolio managers get paid for what amounts to malfeasance."

"I worked in equity investment management for 26 years, owning a firm for 13 of those years and running the firm for 7 years. Our goal as a firm was to beat the S&P 500 Index on a long-term basis. We were successful doing that until the 2000 bear market. The major lesson is 'if you can't beat 'em, join 'em,' causing me to put all equity assets in index funds besides the stock received when the business was sold."

"In the early '90s I allocated all of my 401(k) into an S&P Index fund. Index funds will outperform a majority of the managed funds over the long term, and it takes very little, if any, monitoring on my part."

"Buy index funds—the other stuff is, in some degree, not investing; it's gambling."

"At least until recently, I've been pretty taken with the idea that it's tough to beat the markets in the long term. I'm pretty comfortable putting cash into a Wilshire 5000 Index fund and just hoping it will turn out okay, à la Jonathan Clements in his 'Getting Going' column in the *Wall Street Journal*."

"Thinking a mutual fund manager can beat the market over the long term is wrong. I paid management fees for too long, and for what?"

Index Fund Logic

Several "What Works" investors said index funds are attractive because professional investment managers have a tough time outperforming the market's average return. That's true, but not for the reason many people think. Indexing's relative success is often ascribed to market efficiency. According to the efficient market hypothesis, stock and bond prices always incorporate all available information, so no one can profit from analysis and interpretation of that information. That may or may not be true, but even if the markets weren't efficient, and talented professionals could profit from canny analysis of the available data, indexing would still outperform the average actively managed fund.

The reason is cost. By definition, all investors as a group earn the market's average return. If the U.S. stock market returns 10%, then the combined return of all stock market investors is 10%. Some earn more, some less, but on average, investors earn 10%—before the costs of investing are deducted. After costs, investors earn 10% minus the investment's costs, which might be 1% to 2% of assets. The result is net returns of 8% to 9% for the average actively managed fund.

Index funds vault past the actively managed average by accepting the market average and keeping costs razor thin, as low as 0.20% of assets (or less!). The result is a net return of perhaps 9.8%. So index funds' success relative to actively managed funds does not depend on debatable theories such as the "efficient market hypothesis." It's simply a matter of cost. So long as an index is representative of the securities owned by active managers, the index fund will always outperform the average. Of course, if you believe you can identify in advance the managers who will consistently outperform the market, then indexing has limited appeal.

Bond Mutual Funds or Individual Bonds

Like broad-market stock funds, broadly diversified bond mutual funds offer diversification. This can be especially important when investing in corporate bonds, because companies can go bankrupt and the prices of their bonds can plummet—a risk exemplified during 2002 by telecommunications giant WorldCom. And like stock funds, bond funds can be either actively or passively managed, though the investors we surveyed didn't venture many opinions on one approach to bond investing versus the other.

When evaluating individual bonds versus bond funds, it's important to know that even though both investments play similar roles in a portfolio, they behave differently. Most bond funds maintain a *constant average-weighted maturity*: a short-term bond fund is forever short term, an intermediate-term bond is forever intermediate term, and so on. A bond fund never matures and returns your initial investment. As the bonds within the fund mature, the fund manager simply reinvests the proceeds in new bonds. (You can redeem your bond mutual fund shares at any time, of course, just as you can with any other mutual fund.)

By contrast, individual bonds eventually mature. Their maturities shrink every year until their maturity dates, when they return the value of your principal. This characteristic allows you to know with certainty how much principal will be coming back to you on a specific date in the future. This difference explains why some of our investors preferred individual bonds to bond funds.

> "My worst mistake was investing in bond funds rather than buying bonds. Bond funds have quite a bit of volatility and never mature to refund your initial investment. With bond funds, you could gain or lose depending on when you sell."

> "You are better off buying the individual bonds if you want stability and some income."

> "I invested in zero-coupon bonds, with each one coming due a year after the other, starting in the year I would reach 70½. The rest I invested for retirement. It was a safe investment, and no worries."

When the economy's interest rates rise, the prices of existing bonds fall. When the prevailing level of interest rates falls, the prices of existing bonds rise. Although these inverse movements initially seem confusing, they're very logical. When interest rates rise, new bonds will be issued with higher coupon payments than bonds issued when rates were lower. When interest rates are 5%, a bond with a face value of $1,000 will pay annual coupons equal to $50. If rates rise to 6%, a new bond with the same face value will pay annual coupons of $60. No one would buy the existing bonds unless their prices fell to a level at which their $50 coupons constituted a yield equal to the 6% available from new bonds. How far must the price of the existing bonds fall? At $833, the bond with a $50 coupon will offer a yield of 6% ($50/$833 = 6%), the same yield available from new bonds.

Both bonds and bond mutual funds are subject to these price swings. If you hold individual bonds, however, you don't see the price change, simply because most investors don't calculate the value of their bonds on a daily basis, as a mutual fund must. Plus, if you intend to hold the bond until maturity, any temporary loss or gain in value will disappear by the time the principal is repaid. It's important to note that a rise in rates, and the resulting fall in principal value, can be "good news" for mutual fund investors who are reinvesting their coupon payments. These coupons, plus the principal value of the fund's maturing bonds, can be reinvested at higher interest rates, potentially offsetting the loss of principal sustained by a mutual fund.

A bond fund doesn't aim for stability of principal, but a low-cost bond fund is more practical for many investors. If you're reinvesting your interest payments, funds allow you to do so automatically. Plus, you can reinvest payments that would be too small to allow for the purchase of a new bond, and mutual funds boast the buying power necessary to get the best prices from Wall Street's bond desks. If you're living off the income, mutual funds may also help with budgeting and cash flow. Most funds pay income distributions monthly. Individual bonds make payments just twice a year. Finally, if you're investing in bonds to diversify a stock-heavy portfolio, the bond fund's constant maturity is an advantage. You don't have to worry about rolling maturing bonds into new securities; the fund takes care of it.

Although some of the investors considered individual bonds superior to funds, the portfolios of most respondents did not reflect this. As noted earlier, on average, they keep about 19% of their bond assets in individual bonds and the remainder in bond funds.

Key Considerations for Investing in Bonds

by Ian A. MacKinnon

Until his retirement in June 2003, Ian A. MacKinnon was managing director of Vanguard's Fixed Income Group and was responsible for portfolio management and credit analysis for most of the company's actively managed and indexed bond funds. Mr. MacKinnon joined Vanguard in 1981.

Many investors find decisions about how to invest in bonds even more difficult than deciding how to invest in stocks. Part of the difficulty stems from the fact that owning an individual bond is quite different from owning a fund that invests in bonds.

If you buy stock in a company—say 100 shares of General Electric—what you own today is essentially the same thing you owned 20 years ago. You own a small piece of a company. Yes, GE has changed through the years, but the fundamental nature of a share of stock hasn't changed.

But suppose that 20 years ago you bought a 20-year bond issued by GE. Back then, you had a security that would pay you a set amount of interest each year. Today, that bond has matured and you're holding cash—an entirely different type of asset from a bond.

The passage of time has unique effects on bonds that don't occur for stocks. After one year, that 20-year bond becomes a 19-year bond. After a decade, it's a 10-year bond. And, of course, bonds can change in other ways, too. The creditworthiness of a company and the credit rating of its bonds can rise or fall.

On the other hand, buying a bond fund is in some ways more like buying a stock. The fundamental characteristics of the investment are not likely to change substantially. If you invest in an intermediate-term U.S. Treasury fund with an average maturity of 6 to 10 years, it will still be an intermediate-term Treasury fund a decade from now. Its yield may change over the decade, but the basic risk-reward characteristics of the fund will not change.

Fundamentals of Bond Selection

Both professional bond fund managers and do-it-yourself investors ought to consider the same factors in selecting individual bonds. The most important of these are credit quality and interest rate risk.

We have seen a huge increase in credit risk in recent years. Price fluctuations due to changes in real or perceived credit quality are greater than ever. And you're seeing severe price declines not only for the security whose issuer is really in trouble but in entire industry groups. If one company in an industry is in trouble, it's like an infection—suspicion falls on the other companies in the industry, too. Investors' tolerance for risk is very low, and their confidence in the financial reports of bond issuers is even lower. The credit-rating agencies are more aggressive than they used to be when it comes to changing a bond issuer's credit ratings—they downgrade first and ask questions later.

These bond market developments make it more important than ever to have good credit analysis as well as broad diversification to protect yourself against credit blowups. Given that most individuals aren't in a position to perform extensive credit analysis or to hold hundreds of individual bond issues, those who want to select individual bonds should generally stick to U.S. Treasury and federal government agency bonds.

Treasuries—including inflation-protected bonds—are great investments to own either directly or within a low-cost mutual fund. There are fewer issues to select from, so there are fewer opportunities for a professional manager to add value. For Treasuries, the advantage of a fund is in the efficient reinvestment of income and the proceeds from maturing bonds. The advantage of going it alone is that you can buy Treasuries directly from the government and avoid any commissions and management expenses.

An important, but often overlooked, benefit of bond funds is that fund managers can get significantly better pricing on bond purchases and sales than an individual can. A mutual fund might pay transaction costs of 25 to 35 basis points (0.25% to 0.35%) on a corporate bond purchase, while the individual's costs might be 75 to 150 basis points of the transaction's value. In fact, until you have a portfolio of $10 to $20 million, the costs of buying and selling individual corporate bonds will most likely outweigh the management fees you'd pay in a reasonably priced bond fund. And if you intend to reinvest your bond coupons, the fund's pricing advantages—and convenience—become that much more powerful.

Costs and Taxes

Both stock and bond mutual funds cost money, potentially more than the cost of holding individual securities. Compared with portfolios of individual securities, stock funds can also be a tax headache, though the potential tax benefits of mutual-fund alternatives are often grossly oversold. (Taxes generally aren't much of a factor in comparing bonds and bond funds.) Both funds and investors in individual securities pay transaction costs (brokerage commissions, bid–ask spreads, dealer markups in the case of bonds) when buying securities. (If you trade individual securities, you pay these costs directly. A mutual fund pays these costs on behalf of the fund shareholders.)

Mutual fund shareholders can incur two additional costs. First, some funds levy a sales charge to compensate the broker who sells you the fund. Second, all funds incur ongoing operating costs. Actively managed funds cost more than passively managed (index) funds because, with active management, you have to pay someone to analyze and select investments in an effort to outpace the market averages. Even index funds, which eschew costly investment research, must charge operating expenses to pay for recordkeeping, fund administration, and so on. Mutual fund costs can be exceptionally low, though many funds charge high fees. The "What Works" investors devote more attention to costs in Chapter 8.

Another difference between owning mutual funds and owning individual securities is that with individual securities you retain more control over how and when your investments are taxed. By federal law, a fund must distribute any net capital gains realized when it sells a security—even if you continue to hold your fund shares and even if you reinvest the distribution in the fund. With individual stocks, you decide when—and if—to realize any taxable gains. That control sounds good in theory, but some investors noted that this benefit may ultimately cost you more in trouble than it saves in taxes. Also, a mutual fund that regularly attracts new investors, so that the fund is continually buying new shares of stock at different prices, can provide significant tax-management advantages over a portfolio of securities that is bought at a single point in time. And for the tax-conscious investor, there are additional mutual fund strategies, as explained in Chapter 9. Investors' ambivalence about the tax benefits of holding individual stocks was reflected in a number of comments.

> "With a mutual fund, you can get tagged with gains taxes when someone else sells even if you don't."

> "One thing that you do get with stocks is a deferment of the tax liability, but it's so much easier to invest in mutual funds."

> "I just loathe capital gains distributions. I can't stand the tax decisions being controlled by someone other than me. In my personal portfolio, I tend to do individual stocks. In my IRA, I do funds."

> "My most disappointing experience was buying individual stocks to reduce taxes. Although I picked solid stocks, like Lucent, Qwest, AT&T, AOL, many have lost most of their value."

Advice

Your allocation of stocks, bonds, and cash is the big picture. How you implement that decision (that is, with stocks or stock funds, with bonds or bond funds, with active or passive management) is less important. The "What Works" investors differed over the relative merits of various approaches, but despite quibbling over the nitty-gritty, they agreed on the big things: Invest, diversify, and stick with it.

> "Buy index funds and enjoy life. Rebalance as necessary, given the movement of the stock and bond indexes and the change in

risk profile as one ages—i.e., 80%/20% equity to debt early, 50%/50% in one's sixties, and change according to cash needs after retirement as necessary."

"Establish automatic, regular saving habits. Use a mutual fund for diversification. I like index funds."

"Go with simple long-term index strategy—less stress, better results."

"Buy stock in companies with long-term quality in a business with a future. Buy mutual funds from quality fund companies with no loads and low expenses."

"Manage a portion of your own portfolio. Use index funds. Stay in for the long term. Use no-load funds. Diversify as you approach retirement."

"Know what you don't know, and pick good mutual fund managers to handle diversified investing."

"While building capital, study how the fund operates, which stocks it buys and sells and why. Then venture into individual stock. Also, find good bond funds to balance risk."

"Buy blue chips and hang on. Diversification among stocks, bonds, and cash is important."

In the next chapter, the "What Works" investors move from finance to Freud, and our bedeviling tendency to let emotion sabotage our investment plans. We're all human. As investors, we're all vulnerable to emotion and hard-wired psychological biases that can do damage to our portfolios. The trick is to recognize these weaknesses and adapt.

Different Approaches for Different Investors

by George U. Sauter

George U. Sauter is a managing director at Vanguard and chief investment officer. He is responsible for Vanguard's Quantitative Equity and Fixed Income Groups, which oversee the company's internally managed stock, bond, and money market portfolios. Mr. Sauter joined Vanguard in 1987.

There is no one right approach to the stock market. You can invest 100% of your assets in individual securities, in index funds, or in actively managed funds.

The decision takes place along a risk spectrum, as displayed in Figure 5.2. At the lowest-risk end of the spectrum is a 100% broad-based indexed portfolio, which exposes you only to market risk—the risk, that the entire stock market will decline.

The next-riskiest approach is an actively managed portfolio, in which you get the diversification provided by mutual funds, but you also take on both market risk and manager risk—the risk that your manager will underperform the market or a market benchmark.

At the riskiest end of the spectrum is a portfolio consisting of a single stock or a few stocks. There you're subject not only to market risk but to manager risk and to individual security risk—the risk that a specific security will blow up, perhaps due to a bankruptcy or a crippling lawsuit.

FIGURE 5.2 The spectrum of stock market risk.

Source: The Vanguard Group, Inc.

Individual Stocks: Extraordinary Risk for Extraordinary Goals

If you have $50 billion, you can afford the risk of investing in a concentrated portfolio of individual stocks. If you lose 99% of the portfolio's value, you'll still have $500 million. You're not going to go hungry.

A classic example of this kind of investor might be Microsoft chairman Bill Gates. He's wealthy enough that risk reduction is not an important goal. He may want to maintain a large stake in Microsoft—or become the world's first trillionaire. He probably can't accomplish those goals in an indexed portfolio, or a diversified managed portfolio. Bill Gates can afford extraordinary risk in pursuit of extraordinary goals, but most of us can't.

Several investors indicated that their portfolios are heavily invested in individual stocks. I'd caution that being diversified with individual stocks requires more holdings than most people realize. You cannot gain sufficient diversification with $50,000 and a portfolio of, say, 25 stocks. You probably need at least $1 million and several hundred stocks to gain reasonable diversification.

Active Management: Above-Average Risk and Opportunity

An actively managed approach is completely rational for investors who (1) are willing to assume risk beyond market risk and (2) are able to discern which managers can add value.

You can decide whether you pass the first part of that test by assessing your own risk tolerance and investment biases. Determining whether you pass the second part of the test is difficult, but not impossible. If I were looking for a superior active manager, I'd start with four criteria.

1. The manager's fund must have low costs. Over time, the margins of outperformance, even for the best managers, are so modest that low costs are a must.
2. The manager must have a systematic approach, meaning that he or she follows a clear, logical investment methodology. Without such a framework, you won't know what role the fund plays in your portfolio; plus, there's a risk that the manager will chase whatever is doing well at the moment—a strategy that may work for a time but usually ends in disaster.
3. The manager must have a consistent philosophy that is consistently applied. The strategy must be grounded in some fundamental belief

about how the stock market behaves, and this philosophy must be apparent in the portfolio's management through all cycles of the market. If a manager believes that stocks with low price/book ratios tend to outperform stocks with high price/book ratios over the long run, that belief should be reflected in the way the fund invests, through up and down markets, and in value- and growth-driven markets.

4. The manager must have demonstrated an ability to outperform in the past.

There is strong support for the view that there are stock market inefficiencies that can be exploited by active strategies. In other words, there are smart managers who can identify mispriced stocks and then profit from those mispricings when other investors also recognize the mismatch. The Vanguard Group manages several billion dollars with strategies that attempt to profit from these inefficiencies. But I don't think that most investors appreciate the difficulty of adding value through active management—of beating the market benchmarks. As a whole, active management is a zero-sum game. Any value I can add must come from the returns of another active manager who trails the market benchmark. As a group, we all earn the market return, minus our costs. Even if you're confident that you can identify superior managers, it still makes sense to have a core holding in index funds, complemented by smaller holdings in actively managed funds.

Index Funds: Market Risk

An indexed approach is appropriate for investors who simply want broad-based, low-cost exposure to the stock market. They're willing to assume market risk, but are skeptical that manager risk or individual security risk can reliably generate compensating rewards. This approach is probably suited to far more investors than currently exploit it: Only about 12% of U.S. stock market assets are invested in index funds. Yet theory and experience show that just 20% to 30% of active managers outperform the market over the long haul. And it's very difficult to know—in advance—which managers will do so. Those long odds suggest that investors as a group could enhance their after-cost returns by allocating more assets to the indexed end of the spectrum.

Action Steps

- Honestly assess your personal risk tolerance and your ability to identify winning strategies. This will enable you to find your place on the stock market risk spectrum. There is a trade-off between trying to beat the market and the amount of risk you take.

- Whatever strategy you choose, keep your costs low. In an index fund, low costs are essential in order to match the index results. In an active strategy, low costs maximize your opportunity to benefit from whatever excess returns the strategy generates.

chapter six

AVOID SELF-DESTRUCTIVE MOVES

Developing an investment program is relatively easy, but sticking with it is hard. "All investors are driven by two forces, greed and fear," noted an investor from Ohio, a refrain that was repeated time and again by other respondents. In the Darwinian wild, these powerful emotions may help ensure your survival; in the financial markets, they're a liability. "People get scared when the market goes wild. They end up buying high and selling low," observed one investor.

The "What Works" investors have at times been laid low themselves by these emotional sandbags. "People base buy-and-sell decisions on knee-jerk reactions. Or they buy on a 'hot tip' from a friend," one investor wrote. "They don't have a financial strategy or a plan. No diversification. Investors make these mistakes because they're human. They have human desires such as greed, and they don't want to be bothered by taking time to learn—they're too busy." Sound familiar?

During the past 25 years, academics have developed a new field of inquiry—behavioral finance—to study the psychological biases that can work against us as investors. Their research suggests that we're not the hyperrational utility maximizers who populate classical economic models. Instead, we're human beings. We make emotional decisions that can do damage to our portfolios.

Although this chapter is inspired by the behavioral-finance research, this academic discipline has not explicitly investigated emotionally driven decisions. The research has focused on cognitive biases that are at odds with rational investment behavior. But the experiences of our investors suggest that these hard-wired biases and our emotional responses to the market are simply different paths to the same destination: lousy investment decisions.

In this chapter, investors review their negotiations with greed and fear in bull and bear markets of the past, offering perspective on the importance of a plan when emotion runs high and reason is in retreat. And they offer advice on systematizing the habits and practices that can keep emotion at bay: dollar-cost averaging, rebalancing, simplifying, and indexing.

Greed

The "What Works" investors attributed most investors' counterproductive behaviors to greed and fear. Greed caught most of the blame. Greed compels investors to chase hot-performing stocks and funds, to establish unrealistic expectations for investment returns, and to trade frequently in pursuit of the big score. Chasing performance is one of the most common pitfalls, not just among this set of investors, but among investors generally.

Performance Chasing

> "Unsuccessful investors chase hot sectors or asset classes. Too many people act like they are in Las Vegas. They make this mistake primarily due to greed and herd mentality, rather than analytical factors."

> "I think many investors 'follow the herd' rather than buy things that seem to be good value. Or put another way, they buy investments that are popular rather than those that are likely to produce a good return."

> "The common tendency is to jump in near the top and sell out near the bottom. It's based on emotion, rather than knowledge and analysis."

> "People follow the crowd believing there is strength in numbers. Just because an investment has a meteoric rise doesn't mean it can't have a meteoric fall."

> "My worst experience was [a high-profile Internet fund]. I'm hoping to learn to take my time investing and not rush into something because I'm afraid I'll miss the boat."

> "My worst experience was chasing hot stocks with an aggressive broker from [a major brokerage firm]. The highs and lows of this adventure became a daily game of greed and fear. To practice these two emotions each day was detrimental to my emotional and physical health."

> "Probably the biggest mistake is in investing in the hottest thing at the moment. People do this because they are told, and they believe, that they can make money fast. No real sense of risk-reward balance. They make this mistake because they tend to listen to only a few 'advisers,' typically biased sources who are themselves invested in the stock or venture. They should look for advice from many sources."

It's hard to appreciate the perils of performance chasing until you've spent some time in the market—or listened closely to someone who has. After all, for most big purchases, such as a car, it makes sense to look for a track record of success to find something that will perform well in the future. But as "What Works" investors have learned, in investing, past performance is no guarantee of future results. That's not just boilerplate; it's true. Over time, the performance of different asset classes and market sectors waxes and wanes. By the time an investment reaches the top of the performance tables, there's a good chance that its run is over.

At the end of 1999, the average technology mutual fund reported a sizzling one-year return of 135.5%, almost six times the return of the broad U.S. stock market, according to investment research firm Morningstar. During the next three months, investors poured $33.7 billion into technology funds, more money by far than was invested in any other sector of the stock market during the same period.

From then on, the pickings got lean. In the 12 months through March 31, 2001, the average technology fund returned –61.6%, according to Morningstar, transforming a $10,000 investment into $3,840. One investor, with more than 45 years of investment experience, called his biggest mistake "investing in the tech boom in 1999 and 2000. I should not have changed my value-investment approach to a blend of value and tech. I've learned you should never move to the hot-button stock or area."

Hot Hands Gone Cold

The danger of chasing particular stocks or market sectors also applies to mutual funds. Author and economics professor Burton G. Malkiel identified the 20 mutual funds that performed best from the start of 1990 to the start of 1995, the hot hands of the early 1990s. In the next five years, this elite group fell to the middle of the pack. The fund that had finished first during the first half of the 1990s fell to 129th by the end of the second half. The third-place finisher tumbled to 261st place—almost dead last among the 283 mutual funds that survived the full ten years.[1]

Although it seems to defy the kind of common sense you apply to many decisions in your life, "you can't chase performance like a day-trader," observed a retired investor living in Florida. The past is not prologue.

Although it seems to defy the kind of common sense you apply to many decisions in your life, "you can't chase performance like a day-trader," observed a retired investor living in Florida. The past is not prologue.

Unrealistic Expectations

The "What Works" investors noted that greed can foster unrealistic expectations about investment returns and risks.

Unrealistic expectations pose two risks. First, if you expect unrealistically high returns, you may not save enough to meet your goals. Second, when your high hopes are eventually dashed, the urge to take extreme risks to catch up may prove overpowering.

> "It's that much harder to do the right things if you don't save. If you have less money—define that however you like—if you think you need $1 million at 40, and you have $100,000, you'll do the wrong things. You just will. It's human nature. The guys with the least money are always going for the home run. It seems counterintuitive, because they can least afford the risk."

> One investor noted that too many investors engage in "short-term speculation with long-term money. Not saving early in life. It's a by-product of the get-rich-quick mentality that permeates our culture, whether from state-sponsored lottos or tech hype from Wall Street."

> "When the [2000–2002] bear market began, I was 85% invested in stocks, despite being over 60 years of age. My portfolio is now much more balanced. I learned it doesn't pay to be greedy. I now realize I have enough money to last the rest of my life if I don't get greedy."

> "I was too eager to gain large returns. Kept looking for an economic rebound in late 2000 and early 2001. Should have stuck to a conservative, diversified portfolio and ridden the downturn out."

> "Unsuccessful investors have too much faith, too many dreams."

Frequent Trading

The "What Works" investors cited greed as the cause of another investment ill: frequent trading. Trading costs money in commissions, bid–ask spreads, and sizable opportunity costs if the investments you buy tend to lag the investments you sell, which happens with uncanny frequency. In their paper "Trading Is Hazardous to Your Wealth," professors Brad Barber and Terrance Odean examined the trading records of thousands of investors. From 1991 through 1996, those who traded most earned the lowest returns: an average of 5 percentage points per year less than the broad market average. Part of the shortfall was due to costs and part to the fact that the stocks people sold did better than the ones they bought. "People are overconfident," the authors concluded, "and overconfidence leads to too much trading."[2] Or, as one investor put it, "people are blinded by their instinct and self-confidence."

> "I remember back in 1987, I lost a third of what I had in one day. Shortly afterward, I sold Pfizer, and the darn thing went up fortyfold after that. I was not a smart investor in the late 1980s. I'm sure if I went back and looked, I'd see that I made a lot of mistakes. The first things I bought out of college were a bank stock and a tech stock. Two days after I bought the tech stock, it went bankrupt. I lost $1,000 right away. My dad said that would be a cheap lesson. The boring bank just turned out to be great. The things that sound cool and risky are not as good as the solid, boring companies."

> "My most disappointing experiences were working with a broker in Minneapolis in the 1980s who never talked in terms of asset allocation. I missed a lot of time learning how to invest because of this. Also, doing a lot of trading with stocks I purchased for my child during his growing-up years. If I had simply bought and held stock, or a good mutual fund for him when he was younger, he would be in financially better shape today."

One investor's best decision was "sticking with a 50/50 asset allocation for equities and fixed income and limiting the stock-trading option of my account to a relatively small portion of the total."

Fear

In investing, fear is greed's equally harmful inverse. Greed can prompt you to take foolish and ultimately destructive risks, but fear can sabotage a long-term plan that calls for some exposure to higher-returning, higher-risk, assets. "Unsuccessful investors sell on emotion!" wrote a Maryland woman. "They fear that they may lose everything." Fear can also prevent you from acting to develop the kind of sensible, long-term plan that can help you reach your goals.

"My most disappointing experience was investing in certificates of deposit, thinking that they were a safe vehicle, when I could have been in the stock market sooner if I had not invested in CDs."

"I kept too much of my retirement funds in short-term bond funds in the late '80s/early '90s. I should have been more heavily weighted in stocks."

"I was too conservative. I had too much emphasis on bonds and my money grew too slowly."

Loss Aversion

The source of fear is aversion to loss. Academic research has demonstrated that we hate losing more than we love winning.[3] Because of this bias, certain investment practices can be extremely counterproductive. As our "What Works" investors discovered, excessive monitoring of your portfolio is especially hazardous. Stocks have been more likely to decline in the short term than in the long term. Thus, the more frequently you check a stock portfolio, the more likely you are to see a loss. Our investors urged us to "have patience" and to "hold for the long term." Those phrases are repeated so often that they're easy to ignore, but there's a reason these tips have become clichés.

Investment author William J. Bernstein has calculated that the probability of loss in the stock market has historically been about 50% over a time horizon of one day, as shown in Table 6.1. Over a year, the probability dips to about 30%. Over a ten-year period, the probability tumbles to less than 1%.

In an interview with *Money* magazine, Daniel Kahneman, a behavioral finance pioneer and recipient of the 2002 Nobel Prize in economic sciences, said, "If owning stocks is a long-term project for you, following their changes constantly is a very, very bad idea. It's the worst possible thing you can do, because people are so sensitive to short-term losses. If you count the money every day, you'll be miserable."[4] A number of investors reported spending time on this emotional roller coaster.

TABLE 6.1 Investing Time Horizon and Probability of Loss in the Stock Market

Time horizon	*Probability of loss (%)*
One hour	49.58
One day	48.80
One week	47.36
One month	44.51
One year	30.85
Ten years	0.59
100 years	0

Source: William J. Bernstein, "Of Risk and Myopia," www.efficientfrontier.com/ef/102/taleb.htm.

"Unfortunately, I monitor my portfolio daily. Now that I've retired, I have more time. And you watch CNBC, you watch your account values on the computer. That's too much. You shouldn't be doing that. But when you're on a retirement income, you get a little anxious. You can't help it. It's human nature."

"People spend too much time monitoring their investments. I have watched people narrow their interests in life to producing, consuming, and conserving their wealth, and allowing other interests to wither. The 'more' and 'better' push is a contagious message of our society and is hard to resist when so many of your dinner guests excuse themselves early to check the markets."

"People spend too much time monitoring their investments. I have watched people narrow their interests in life to producing, consuming, and conserving their wealth, and allowing other interests to wither. The 'more' and 'better' push is a contagious message of our society and is hard to resist."

On average, our investors reviewed their portfolios 88 times a year, about every four days or so. Some 72% of respondents checked their portfolios at least monthly; the remainder checked quarterly or less. Quarterly may not seem excessive, but even four looks a year may be too much for some people. "When the statements come we look at them," one woman told us, "and then we die a little, and then we hope it will go back up." A small group of investors—just 5%—checked their portfolios once a year or less, and a few of these respondents suggested that checking infrequently gives them a healthy perspective on the market's ups and downs.

> "I usually wind up checking the portfolio at the same time that I do my taxes. I get calls from one of these so-called investment advisers. He started to give me all this razzmatazz about how much money I'd lost, and I told him 'I haven't lost anything because I haven't sold anything.' Of course, I haven't made anything over the last few years, either, for the same reason. That really threw him for a loop."

> "I bought an IRA with a balanced fund and then I'm managing a trust for my daughter, which had some individual stocks and a money market fund, and then I'm managing another trust, and I don't want to have to manage it actively, so I bought five different funds that are all tax-managed. Because that one's long term for my grandson, I don't need to manage it. I'm just riding with the market with a 20-year outlook. I dislike very much looking at the market. The reason I've got tracking [index] funds is that from what I read, over the long haul, even the funds that are in certain sectors don't outperform the market. Let the market do the work."

Fighting the Enemy Within

To combat counterproductive emotions, our seasoned investors offered a number of nuts-and-bolts suggestions for automating the practices that keep a sensible long-term plan on track: dollar-cost averaging, rebalancing, simplifying, and indexing. Of course, these strategies presume that you have a plan. You can't systematize the actions necessary to execute your plan if the plan doesn't exist. Other respondents advocated, to the extent possible, cultivating a cast of mind that helps you to keep focused on your goals. Here are their ideas for keeping things on an even keel.

Dollar-Cost Averaging. *Dollar-cost averaging* is an industry term for the simple practice of investing a set amount of money in the market on a regular basis, regardless of whether the markets are climbing or falling.

You buy fewer shares when prices are high, more when prices are low. Dollar-cost averaging doesn't ensure a profit or protect you against a loss in declining markets, nor will it prevent a loss if you stop dollar-cost averaging when the value of your account is less than your cost. Before adopting this method, you should consider your willingness and ability to invest continually, even through periods of market decline, since the advantages of dollar-cost averaging depend on your making regular purchases through thick and thin. In a sense, though, the point of dollar-cost averaging is that you don't have to consider your resolve during the tough times. By investing automatically, you remove emotion from the equation.

> "Use mutual funds. Diversify. Buy T-bills. Make monthly regular contributions of equal amounts to each fund. Don't watch the stock market more often than every quarter. Ignore what everybody knows and never panic."
>
> One investor's best experience was "participating in DRIPs [dividend reinvestment plans]. Choosing to have dividends paid in additional shares rather than in cash enabled me to accumulate shares of stock (dollar-cost averaging) without paying a lot of attention to share prices. Over the years, the number of shares I own has increased dramatically."
>
> "Crawl, walk, run to a mutual fund, and do it not in a lump sum, but by regular periodic contributions."
>
> "Don't try to beat the market. Try and be part of the market. Dollar-cost average. Diversify. Low costs. Long-term timeframe. Don't get spooked."
>
> "Use dollar-cost averaging and buy and hold. Have sufficient cash assets that you don't need to sell into a down market."
>
> "Dollar-cost averaging is the ultimate weapon against emotional investing."

Rebalancing. Restoring your stock, bond, and cash allocations at regular intervals to the target allocations set out in your investment plan is known as rebalancing. Rebalancing can mean buying stocks (or bonds) when prices are tumbling, and your stock (or bond) ratio has shrunken, or selling stocks (or bonds) when they're on fire and your ratio has ballooned. These counterintuitive moves can be emotionally tough, but by systematizing this discipline, you keep your portfolio's risk level and return prospects in line with those set out in your plan. You may even reap a rebalancing bonus from buying low and selling high, but that certainly can't be counted on.

> "Successful investors have the patience to wait out market fluctuations. They take care in analyzing past performance. They know the true cost of investing. They follow their portfolios and rebalance when appropriate."

> "Diversify. Watch fees. Don't worry about day-to-day ups and downs. Invest early and regularly. Rebalance every two years."

> "Successful investors research investment choices, invest regularly, monitor their selections, rebalance periodically, make choices based on their risk tolerance. Unsuccessful ones buy and sell on whims, take action at inappropriate times, and do not take time to do research."

Simplifying and Indexing. Simplifying and indexing reduce the number of decisions you have to make. The fewer decisions you make, the fewer opportunities emotion has to wreck your plan. "All of us," Professor Kahneman told *Money*, "would be better investors if we just made fewer decisions."[5] Some investors advocated index funds as a simple way to invest. Index funds simply aim to track the returns of market indexes. They eliminate the need to make judgments about a particular stock or mutual fund manager. Index funds might solve the dilemma articulated by a California investor: "Because of my engineering background, I suffer a bit of analysis paralysis. Today there's just too much to read and there's an excessive number of funds and fund companies."

> "I've tried to shift at least half the money I have into index funds. I'm trying to eliminate some of the funds I have. I'm not sure why I have them. And I will probably move those to index funds—for diversification reasons, and it's probably safer. Keeps the costs down, and I basically know where everything is just by listening to the news reports on the markets."

> "If I had to do it over again, I would take index funds—large-caps, small-caps, and mid-caps—get three funds and have it over with."

> "My most successful experience has been investing in index funds. I learned that I can do well without too much worry."

Don't Just Do Something, Sit There!

"Do 'couch potato' allocation," advised one investor. Although this Texan has accumulated a sizable portfolio, his advice can be followed easily by the rawest investor of the most modest means. The reference is to an investment approach popularized by *Dallas Morning News* columnist Scott Burns: "It is a portfolio designed for people who want to approach their investments with the calm of Yoda, the Buddha-like instructor of young Jedi," Burns explained. "The Couch Potato Portfolio is simple, inexpensive, unmanaged, and devoid of hubris."[6] Burns's formula consisted of a 50/50 mix of a stock index fund and a bond index fund, to be rebalanced once a year and ignored for the other 364 days. Aggressive couch potatoes might consider a 75/25 combination of stocks and bonds.

Over the 1-, 3-, 5-, 10-, and 15-year periods ended May 30, 2002, Burns reported, the couch potatoes fared commendably relative to their energetic counterparts. Burns's findings are presented in Table 6.2.

TABLE 6.2 Couch Potato Portfolios versus Balanced and Domestic Equity Funds (Annualized returns for periods ended May 30, 2002)

Period	*50%/50% CP*[a]	*75%/25% CP*[b]	*Average balanced*	*Average domestic equity*
1 year	–1.80%	–6.91%	–4.01%	–11.32%
3 years	2.89	1.22	2.21	3.33
5 years	9.66	10.29	7.01	8.72
10 years	10.37	11.68	8.98	11.27
15 years	10.96	12.30	9.45	11.85

Source: Scott Burns, "Revising the Couch Potato Portfolio," *Dallas Morning News*, September 30, 2002.

[a]Couch potato portfolio: 50% of assets in Vanguard® 500 Index Fund, 50% in Vanguard® Total Bond Market Fund.

[b]Couch potato portfolio: 75% of assets in Vanguard® 500 Index Fund, 25% in Vanguard® Total Bond Market Fund.

Cultivating the Right Cast of Mind. These simple nuts-and-bolts tactics can go a long way toward keeping emotion out of the picture. But developing the right perspective is also important. The investors in our survey suggested some productive ways to look at and respond to the markets' movements.

> "Our best experience was putting money in our 401(k) and not paying too much attention to it. I learned if you put your money in a reasonably sound investment and forgot about it, it would do better than constantly tinkering with it."

> "Buy mutual funds and stay put. Keep buying and don't watch too closely (it's too scary)."

> "Too much emphasis is placed on the hot funds and the hot stocks. If a fund or a stock is making headlines, it should be avoided."

"The market can be very volatile. Have a long-range plan and stick to it. Don't make big decisions based on short-term results."

"Limit the percentage of individual stocks. Invest mostly in mutual funds. Utilize index funds. Keep portfolio to less than 15–20 funds. Diversify."

"Avoid trendy investments. Buy and hold good mutual funds. Make regular investments and reinvest your dividends."

"Be unemotional. Don't get excited at the top and buy. Don't get depressed at the bottom and sell."

Ultimately, setting a goal, developing an appropriate asset allocation, and selecting a handful of funds are not hugely complex tasks. The hard part comes next: battling your emotions so that you can stick with your plan through thick and thin.

In this chapter, the investors offer tips, both tactical and psychological, on fighting the enemy within. In the next chapter, they discuss some gauges to consider as you monitor an investment plan. By keeping the focus on your plan's progress toward your goals, you can tune out the incessant noise that causes so much trouble.

Be Aware of Your Biases

by Stephen P. Utkus

Stephen P. Utkus, a principal, directs Vanguard's Center for Retirement Research, which produces reports for plan sponsors, consultants, and policymakers; conducts primary research on the savings and investment behavior of U.S. workers; and collaborates with leading academic and industry researchers on areas of mutual interest. Mr. Utkus joined Vanguard in 1987.

Behavioral-finance research reveals differences between the way we actually make decisions and the way those decisions should be made according to classical models of rational economic behavior. These behavioral biases aren't inherently good or bad—they're rooted in human nature—but they generally work against us as investors. The trick is to recognize your biases and work with them, or guard against them.

Inertia

One of the great challenges in investing is overcoming inertia. You've got to start. You've got to take positive steps to start saving or investing. Many of our survey respondents recommended periodic saving (or dollar-cost averaging). I like that advice, especially if the savings are automatically deducted from your paycheck or bank account, because a regular savings program puts inertia to work for you. Once you start saving, you're unlikely to stop. The downside is that you may not increase your savings rate as your income and future needs increase. If you earn $25,000 a year and start saving $50 a month, chances are you'll still be saving $50 a month even if your income triples.

The Center for Retirement Research at Vanguard is studying a program for retirement plans that would automatically increase peoples' savings rate with each pay raise. When you sign up, you agree to increase your savings rate by, say, 1 or 2 percentage points when your pay rises at some point in the future. And because of inertia, the thinking goes, you'll be unlikely to take steps to scale back those future increases. The early results are promising, but most investors don't yet have access to these programs. A do-it-yourself alternative is to incorporate periodic savings increases into your investment plan. Once a year when you assess your portfolio and maybe rebalance, your plan could dictate an increase in your savings tied to any merit or cost-of-living increase in your salary. If you make this increase a formal part of your plan, you may improve your likelihood of following through.

Overconfidence

Many studies have found that people tend to be overconfident about their ability in many endeavors, from driving a car to investing. Excessive trading of investments and overestimating the returns we can earn are examples of our tendency to overrate our abilities. It's interesting that several investors noted stocks they sold that went on to perform better than the investments they bought in their place. The academic research has found the same results among investors generally. When we trade, we're more likely to make bad trades than good.

About a year ago, we did a survey of 401(k) plan participants, asking about their expectations for financial-market returns. Half of the respondents were expecting a stock market return of 15% or more a year over the next two decades. History—and simple math—suggest that long-term returns will probably be more like 8% to 11% annually. Nearly one-fourth of respondents expected returns of 30% to 100% per year. If you have unrealistic expectations about returns, there's real danger that you won't save enough to reach your goals.

Some researchers think that overconfidence may be a reflection of the fact that people are poor statisticians. Human beings' statistical faculty evolved on the savanna, when we could make sense of the world on ten fingers. We're not wired for complex activities like investing. Why do so many people put a bunch of money in a single stock? Because it has gone up in the past. We see a pattern that isn't there. Being quick to recognize patterns, like where antelope are likely to graze or lions to prowl, is a useful survival skill, but it can lead to statistical and investment errors. If we flip seven heads in a row, we're sure that the next flip will be tails, even though there's a 50/50 probability that the next flip will be heads. We're inherently poor statisticians.

Decision Framing

Behavioral-finance research also tells us that the way a decision is framed can determine the outcome. For example, if you ask a group of people, "Do you want to join your 401(k) plan?" 60% of them may say yes. But if you say, "You're joining unless you opt out," you'll get higher enrollment. The question is essentially the same—"Do you want to save?"—but how it's framed determines people's response.

The same thing is clear in asset-allocation decisions. People invest more in stocks if they're presented with annualized returns over 30-year periods rather than the more volatile short-term returns. This tendency shows us why the "What Works" investors' advice to focus on the long term is potentially so powerful. It allows you to frame your allocation decisions in a way that permits you to take the kinds of risks that most of us need to take to meet our long-term goals.

Action Steps

- Be aware of your biases, and make them work for you, not against you.
- Take advantage of inertia by building automatic savings plans and scheduled savings increases into your investment program.
- Beware of overconfidence. Modest expectations and buy-and-hold, broadly diversified strategies limit your vulnerability to the dangers of overconfidence, such as frequent trading or overemphasizing one stock.
- Frame decisions in a way that leads to productive behavior. For example, don't ask, "What can I give up to save more?" Ask, "What can I do to build financial security and freedom for the future?"

chapter seven

ASSESS YOUR PROGRESS

Although the behavioral-finance research suggests that paying excessive attention to your portfolio is usually counterproductive, reaching your goal demands some attention to your progress.

The "What Works" investors used a range of portfolio-tracking methods and tools. Some of their methods were simple. "My goal was to have more next year than last year. Progress tracking is simple." Other investors compared the performance of their portfolios to that of external benchmarks, such as the S&P 500 Index. Some people with large allocations to individual stocks maintained elaborate spreadsheets of their holdings. A few investors relied on methods that incorporated sophisticated financial-planning concepts such as "calculating the annuity that could be purchased with the portfolio's assets." (A fixed, immediate annuity is an insurance product that provides a guaranteed income in exchange for a lump-sum investment.)

How you monitor your portfolio depends on your mix of investments, but the most useful way to analyze performance is within the context of your plan; that is, in accordance with your goals, time horizon, and tolerance for risk. Periodic performance reviews let you know whether you're on track or whether a midcourse correction is in order.

In this chapter, the investors tell us how they evaluate their investment programs and the stocks, bonds, and mutual funds that make up their portfolios. Some of their measures are very different from the yardsticks used in the investment industry and media. The respondents also offer advice on making your periodic evaluations as simple and productive as possible.

Dollars, Rates of Return, and Benchmarks

Among the "What Works" investors, common measuring sticks were specific dollar goals, a target rate of return, or the returns of a financial market index. "My first goal was to accumulate $1 million," said a 75-year-old retiree from California. "I set aside a sum each quarter to meet my goal. Within my established time schedule, I exceeded the goal." A dollar figure as a benchmark boasts the virtues of simplicity and clear relevance to your plan. What matters most is reaching your goal, not matching or beating a market benchmark. Using a simple dollar figure as a target gives you a good sense of the likelihood that you'll be able to pay for your goals, but it may not reveal much about the performance of your investments. After all, if you hope to accumulate $1 million, you could obviously do so by saving $2 million and losing $1 million.

> "My goal is to see a portfolio worth at least $250,000 by 2006. As long as the '90s market went up, all was well."

> "My goal was to eventually have $100,000 in my IRA, as well as other investments, to supplement my pension and social security income. My IRA at one time was worth $69,000. Today it is worth $38,000. My municipal bond investments have provided a steady income, but my limited partnerships have faltered over the past two years."

> "I started a 401(k) when it became available. I did not know the earning potential. I invested the maximum amount I could. As my investments grew, I set a target of $500,000. Unfortunately, the market went down, and I missed by $40,000. I was 80% in stock and 20% bonds."

> "My goal was to make $1 million. Did it."

Some people judged the performance of their investments relative to the returns available from savings options that might or might not be close analogs. For example, a few investors compared the returns of high-risk, potentially high-reward investments, such as stocks, with those of super-safe, U.S. government-insured vehicles, such as CDs. This is comparing apples to oranges. But the fine points of benchmarking may matter more to financial professionals than to investors evaluating their success in selecting among the variety of savings and investment vehicles available to them.

> "My goal was to have more money than if I had left deposits in a CD. If CDs were yielding 7%, I felt I met my goal if my assets returned more than 7%."

> "I began investing in 1951. The goal was to get a better return than I could get in a bank or in savings bonds. I was able to accomplish my goal."

> "It was around 1979. Jimmy Carter was president. The interest rates were 21%. I looked at this savings account we had, this horrible awful savings account, which was getting 5%. The first thing I did was open a money market account with Vanguard. Then later I opened an account in Magellan [Fidelity Magellan Fund, a stock fund]."

Some investors relied on stock and bond market benchmarks, tools widely used within the investment industry. At the most general level, investors might compare the performance of a broadly diversified stock portfolio with that of a broad stock market benchmark, such as the S&P 500 Index or the Wilshire 5000 Index. Or they might measure the performance of their taxable bond portfolio against a broad market gauge like the Lehman Aggregate Bond Index. (A description of the broad market indexes appears in Chapter 4.)

"My goal was to let compound interest work for me over 35–40 years. Assessed progress by comparing results with S&P 500 Index or other yardsticks."

"At the beginning, income from appreciation and yield were most important. That is true today. Today, my benchmark is the S&P 500, but merely following—up and down—is not good enough. The goal is always to do better than the market, keep risk low, and attain good yield and price appreciation."

"My portfolio more or less tracks the market, though it has a higher yield."

If you've chosen to invest in a portfolio that doesn't resemble the broad market, these benchmarks may be inappropriate. For example, if you invest mainly in value-oriented stock funds—those emphasizing stocks with high dividend yields and low ratios of price to earnings (called the price/earnings ratio, or P/E), price to book value, and other corporate measures—your portfolio will perform differently from the S&P 500 Index. The index includes both value *and* growth stocks—stocks with rapid earnings growth and high ratios of price to corporate fundamentals. If you want to determine whether your value funds are providing good performance relative to comparable investments, you'll need to use a specialized value-oriented benchmark, such as the Russell 1000 Value Index.

Specialized Benchmarks

In addition to indexes that track the broad stock and bond markets, there are specialized benchmarks that track the returns of discrete market sectors. If your fund or portfolio of stocks has a pronounced orientation toward a certain style of investing, a specialized benchmark might be the best measuring stick of your investments' relative performance. Table 7.1 lists benchmarks that can help you evaluate the performance of investments with specialized characteristics. Under investment style, *large*, *medium*, and *small* refer to the size of the companies, as measured by the total market value of their shares outstanding (market capitalization). *Growth* and *value* refer to the stocks' fundamental investment characteristics.

TABLE 7.1 Investment Style and Corresponding Benchmarks

Investment style	*Appropriate benchmarks*
Broadly diversified value stocks	Russell 3000 Value Index
Large value stocks	Russell 1000 Value Index, S&P 500/Barra Value Index
Medium value stocks	Russell Midcap Value Index, S&P MidCap 400/Barra Value Index
Small value stocks	Russell 2000 Value Index, S&P SmallCap 600/Barra Value Index
Broadly diversified growth stocks	Russell 3000 Growth Index
Large growth stocks	Russell 1000 Growth Index, S&P 500/Barra Growth Index
Medium growth stocks	Russell Midcap Growth Index, S&P MidCap 400/Barra Growth Index
Small growth stocks	Russell 2000 Growth Index, S&P SmallCap 600/Barra Growth Index

Source: The Vanguard Group, Inc.

This kind of benchmarking can get complicated quickly. Investment research firms such as Morningstar and Lipper can help you make appropriate comparisons. So can fund companies. In fact, for most people, the fund company is the best resource. A mutual fund's prospectus and annual report are required by law to show the performance of the fund relative to an appropriate benchmark.

"Don't invest unless you fully understand what it is you're investing in and understand enough to monitor and evaluate the results, which should be in accordance with why you invested in the first place," explained a semi-retired engineer. The risk of using the wrong benchmark is that you'll draw the wrong conclusion and make a bad investment decision.

Vanguard Chairman Jack Brennan tells a story that illustrates the real-world costs of using faulty benchmarks. During the growth-stock mania of the late 1990s, a shareholder wrote to complain about the performance of Vanguard® Windsor™ II Fund, a large-value fund. Windsor II's returns lagged the stunning returns posted by the broad market indexes and, in particular, the returns of growth funds packed with technology stocks. Table 7.2 shows the returns of both Windsor II and the S&P 500 Index from 1996 through 1999.

When the market and, more notably, growth funds, were posting some of their best returns in history, Windsor II Fund looked pretty shabby. As a large-cap value fund, however, it was doing fine. Windsor II stuck to its strategy of investing in stocks with relatively high dividend yields and low prices relative to company profits, and it beat the vast majority of its large-value competitors in 1996, 1997, and 1998 (but lagged badly in 1999), as shown in Table 7.3.

But Windsor II's strength among the market weaklings wasn't good enough for this shareholder. He cashed out at the end of 1999 and plowed the proceeds into Vanguard® U.S. Growth Fund, which had returned an average of 28.4% a year from 1996 to 1999. That's 2 percentage points per year more than the S&P 500 Index, and a stunning 12.5 percentage points *per year* more than Windsor II, over the same period.

TABLE 7.2 Inappropriate Comparison: Value Versus the Growth-Oriented Market During 1996–1999 (Total returns in %)

	1996	*1997*	*1998*	*1999*
Vanguard Windsor II Fund	24.2	32.4	16.4	–5.8
S&P 500 Index	23.0	33.4	28.6	21.0
Windsor II relative to S&P 500 Index	+1.2	–1.0	–12.2	–26.8

Source: The Vanguard Group, Inc.

TABLE 7.3 Appropriate Comparison: Value Versus Value During 1996–1999 (Total returns in %)

	1996	*1997*	*1998*	*1999*
Vanguard Windsor II Fund	24.2	32.4	16.4	–5.8
Relative to average large-cap value fund	+3.9	+5.2	+4.6	–11.3
Percentage of large-cap value funds outperformed by Windsor II	81.0	89.0	77.0	5.0

Sources: The Vanguard Group, Inc.; Morningstar, Inc.

The timing was horrendous. From January 2000 to December 2001, high-flying growth stocks plummeted. Vanguard U.S. Growth Fund was hit especially hard. The shareholder's $200,000 investment shriveled to $109,060. Had he evaluated Windsor II Fund according to the right benchmarks and stayed the course, his $200,000 would have grown to $225,780. This shareholder's experience illustrates a number of lessons, including the perils of performance chasing, the need to stick with a plan, and the need to hold a diversified portfolio of growth and value stocks. It also highlights the potentially high costs of using the wrong benchmark.

> "I invested $10,000 in a GNMA fund in 1997 without having a good understanding of how bonds work. I withdrew the $10,000 when it appeared I wasn't getting a satisfactory return. When I did move 80% of my retirement money into a money market fund, I could have housed it in the GNMA fund 1½ years ago and made more money. My experience in GNMA kept me from doing that."

Monitoring is trickier with individual stocks. Unless you have a portfolio of many different stocks, diversified benchmarks aren't relevant. And although it's wise to hold a carefully chosen mutual fund more or less indefinitely, the same can't be said of individual stocks (or even bonds): Businesses change, companies are taken over, divisions are spun off. Investing in stocks demands careful attention to corporate fundamentals. Some "What Works" investors noted that if you invest heavily in individual stocks, it's important to have a selling strategy, which introduces a new set of complications. Do you sell based on fundamentals (that is, by analyzing a company's financial statements and earnings prospects)? Or on simple movements in the stock price? The "What Works" investors did both.

> "One thing I'm learning through all of this [bear market] is to have a good selling strategy. I'm kind of angry at myself. I have about 10 to 15 large-cap stocks. I've held them about four years, so some of them had made a lot of money, and even though I had a stockbroker, he never once called me to say, 'Hey, let's button down some of these gains.' Now I can't sell because the loss is so extreme. You have to hope that you're young enough for it to come back."

> "I bought a company stock but did not know when to sell it. The price was falling every time I looked at the stock price on my computer. Know when to sell, have a set price in mind, and sell."

> "Take profits on the way up. Sell half on every double."

> "I am retired from AT&T after 37 years of service. I had acquired AT&T and Baby Bell stock throughout those years. I've never planned to sell them, but I thought the dividends were good for my retirement. Who would have thought AT&T and Lucent would be so disappointing? I suppose I held onto the stocks in all of them because I felt some personal attachment with them. I know now that's not a good investment strategy!"

"My best experience was buying Charles Schwab stock and selling at different time periods, and using the profit to buy more stocks in different companies. Always take some profit when a stock goes up, because you can wait too long to take a profit and the stock price will fall."

"In individual stocks, my biggest mistake was not selling when the stock price reached a level where I clearly would have made a substantial profit."

"I have invested in lots of 'dogs,' and unfortunately, I held on to them too long. Some went down to zero and disappeared. The lesson: Learn to spot a dog while it is still a pup."

"I have invested in lots of 'dogs,' and unfortunately, I held on to them too long. Some went down to zero and disappeared. The lesson: Learn to spot a dog while it is still a pup."

"My best experience was buying individual companies—particularly 'distressed,' 'out-of-favor,' or 'beaten-down' companies—and realizing substantial gains when their businesses improved. Two out of 42 we purchased in this manner (over 27 years) went bankrupt. The remaining 40 all returned more than the S&P 500 Index over their holding period(s). Belief in American companies' ability to recover from adversity will generally be rewarded."

"My most disappointing experience was not selling Broadcom at $200 after buying it at $125 three months earlier. Know when to sell and take profit on tech stocks."

Keeping Records and Tracking Your Holdings

Not long ago, there weren't many ways to monitor a portfolio. You got your mutual fund or brokerage statements and took a peek, or kept an accounting by hand in a ruled ledger. The digital revolution created dozens of new portfolio-tracking tools, some useful, some confusing.

> "I started following more stocks than I was investing in once I got a PC. I think this has been a real asset. I update all my holdings weekly."

> "I rely on Quicken. I use Quicken to keep track of my cost basis. I review my portfolio at least every quarter."

> "I have everything in separate notebooks, so everything is filed away, I've gotten very organized. I have separate notebooks for IRAs, 401(k)s, nonqualified investments, real estate. I keep all the historical documents. It's better for tax planning."

> "Initially, I had no specific goals other than to save for the future. Retirement seemed a long way off. In fact, I did not pay enough attention to my progress and did not maintain a regular investment schedule. Some years later, I became aware of other investment opportunities and got serious about making up for lost time. I became, and still am, a fanatic about keeping accurate records and measuring my progress."

Good records can help you make sense of the holdings you have and how they're performing. A good recordkeeping program doesn't have to be complex. The more holdings you have, the more helpful it may be to use sophisticated computer-based tools that can slice and dice your portfolio in a million different ways, but they're not necessary. "Basically the newspaper," said one millionaire when asked how he keeps up with his portfolio.

He's not alone. As noted in Chapter 3, the "What Works" investors rely on the financial pages of the newspaper for investment news and information more than twice as much as the Internet and three to four times as much as magazines and television.

Our survey respondents also reported checking their portfolios frequently (see Chapter 6), a practice that can be tough on the emotions. On balance, however, these frequent checks haven't led to frequent changes. "I monitored my portfolio monthly, corrected yearly," said one investor, a routine typical of the investors we surveyed.

Table 7.4 shows that only 16% of investors change their portfolios more than once a year. The largest group makes modifications according to no set schedule. We don't know whether that means every five years or every five minutes, but the next-largest groups make changes once a year or less. Research conducted by the Vanguard Center for Retirement Research has found that, like our survey respondents, participants in Vanguard-administered retirement plans tend to stick with their portfolios. In 2001, only 14% of participants made a change in their existing holdings (in 2000, the figure was 17%), and very few made changes in the way future plan contributions were allocated.[1]

The "What Works" investors offered additional advice on strategies for monitoring their investment programs. Some noted that

TABLE 7.4 How Often Do You Change Your Investment Plan? (Percentage of 'What Works' respondents)

Daily	0
Weekly	1
Monthly	4
Quarterly	11
Annually	21
Less frequently	18
No set schedule	45

Source: The Vanguard Group, Inc.

consolidating their assets with one investment company simplifies the task. This advice obviously doesn't apply to alternative assets, such as real estate, but most brokerages and mutual fund companies make it easy to keep your liquid investment assets under one roof. A few people advocated index funds, whose performance demands virtually no oversight. Hard-core stock pickers advised the use of data-heavy analytical tools and sophisticated trading platforms. The key is to develop a system suited to your investment selections and inclinations.

> "Reduce the number of funds. Keep them in the same fund family or company and don't change very often. Stay the course."

> "Consolidating all investments with one company simplifies management, recordkeeping, and monitoring of performance."

> "Over the longer term, I think one of the wisest things I did was to get all my investments in one place. I realize there are pros and cons to this, but I believe the positives for me overcome the negatives."

> "Access to Internet accounts is important. This allows you to obtain real-time quotes and other information such as P/E ratios, dividends. Real-time quotes permit you to obtain a very close look at stock fluctuations to get the best price when you decide to sell. You don't need to wait to read what the price of your stock is in the paper!"

> "Establish or purchase a spreadsheet that will outline budget and total investment portfolio. Use for planning goals. Save as much as possible: IRA, 401(k), taxable investments. Keep it simple and diversify among asset classes (stocks, bonds, cash). Use index funds, low-cost mutual funds. Invest for different time horizons: long-, intermediate-, short-term."

Once you've instituted an investment plan, periodic monitoring of your portfolio can help ensure that your plan remains on track. If the performance of the financial markets gives your portfolio an asset mix that differs from your target allocation, you'll know what you need to do to rebalance your holdings to their original proportions. The "What Works" investors rely on a number of methods to monitor their portfolios. The method that's right for you depends both on the investments used to implement your plan and on the amount of oversight you wish to exercise.

The "What Works" investors next discuss an element of investment selection so important that it gets its own chapter. Although costs get relatively little attention in the investment community at large, our survey respondents cited them as the single most important criterion for selecting an investment provider.

Monitoring Your Portfolio and Its Components

by Jeffrey S. Molitor

Jeffrey S. Molitor, a principal, directs Vanguard's Portfolio Review Group, overseeing the performance and monitoring of Vanguard mutual funds. A Chartered Financial Analyst, he joined Vanguard in 1987.

There are really two levels of review for your investments. First, you assess the performance of your aggregate portfolio. How is it doing as a whole? Then you evaluate the performance of the portfolio's components. The first level of analysis is more important, but, paradoxically, the second is more complicated.

Is Your Portfolio Consistent with Your Goals?

When you're looking at your portfolio as a whole, you need to ask whether your asset allocation is consistent with your goals and time horizon. Because you probably have more than one goal, with differing time horizons, consider setting up different "mental buckets" for different goals. In the bucket for critical but longer-term goals, such as retirement, you'll generally have a relatively high allocation to stocks. In the bucket for short-term goals, such as this year's college tuition or property taxes, money market and short-term bond funds make more sense.

If you have the right asset mixes for the right goals, you can set a standard for helping to ensure that your portfolio is doing what you set it up to do. Then it's simply a question of assessing your progress periodically. Some "What Works" investors set standards such as "reach $1 million by 'X' date" or achieving a particular average rate of return. That's okay, but only if you have realistic expectations to start with. If long-term stock returns are going to be about 8% to 11% per year, as they have been in the past, and bonds are expected to return, say 5% to 7%, you can't expect to earn 15% a year in a balanced stock/bond portfolio. And over any reasonable time horizon, you can't accumulate $1 million by saving only $25 a month.

Are the Components Playing Their Roles?

When you're looking at a particular mutual fund or stock, start by asking, "How did that part of the investment world do?" and "Is that performance consistent with my goal for these assets?" If you're in a money market fund, you saw yields drop from a 5% annual rate in mid-2001 to below 1.5% at the end of 2002. That's disappointing, but it was consistent with the fund's objective to hold short-term securities to maintain a stable net asset value. If *stability of principal* was your objective, you chose the right investment. If you were looking for *stable income*, you chose the wrong fund; a long-term, high-quality bond fund would have been more appropriate. The point is that you want to make sure that a fund's characteristics are consistent with what you want the fund to do. Be aware of a fund's potential for changes in share price and income. Be aware of its objective, such as generating high current income, or tracking an index. Then evaluate the fund on that basis.

If you're evaluating an index fund, the process is simple: You want to see if its performance is in line with its target index. If the target index was down, don't be disappointed that the fund was down, too—tracking the index is what it's supposed to do. To evaluate actively managed funds, you can start by checking performance against a market index, but many of these benchmarks are imperfect, and managers are generally not targeting any specific index standard at any one point in time. So, although a fund manager may have a goal of outperforming the S&P 500 Index, he or she may pay little attention to whether the fund's securities resemble those of the index. It's also important to review a fund manager's performance over a variety of time periods, such as one, three, and five years and in different market environments—up markets and down, value- and growth-driven markets, and so on.

At most fund companies, the best way to evaluate your active funds is to read the fund's annual report. Ideally, the report should provide candid, lucid assessments of the market overall, of the market segment on which your fund focuses, and of the performance of the manager who is investing your assets.

At Vanguard, we assess managers from a number of perspectives. It requires a lot of effort. There are no clear rules, and you have to look at the fund from different perspectives. We look at a fund's performance relative to broad market benchmarks as well as to narrower style indexes, such as those based on growth- or value-oriented stocks. We look at the portfolio's characteristics. We do performance-based style assessments (How did the fund's return differ from that of style indexes and peer groups?), holdings-based assessments (Which holdings of a fund differ from those in a benchmark index?), factor-based assessments (Did fund performance differ from an index because of industry weightings or individual stock selections?). This is more analysis than virtually any individual investor has the time or resources to do, and the best summary we have of all these efforts is the fund's annual report. It's not a sanitized view, but a useful way to look at the fund.

Individual Stocks

Just like any professional investor, people who own individual stocks need to continually ask themselves, "Why do I own this stock? For growth? For income? Am I optimistic about the business?" As pointed out by a "What Works" investor, there's probably no better example of why this is critical than investors who 25 years ago owned AT&T. The pieces they owned out of that company's breakup in the mid-1980s have gone in very different directions. For example, BellSouth is more aligned with a traditional regulated phone-service provider. Lucent, another piece of the old AT&T, is in the much riskier telecommunications-equipment business. Companies change. Things change. Make sure you're aware of what's going on.

For every stock you own, it's a good idea to list one to three reasons you like that company and want to own it. These are the sources of your conviction. And if they go away, maybe the reason for owning the stock goes away. To be really diligent, also write down one or two reasons for concern—something apparent, or something that could happen—that would make the stock less attractive. If that comes to pass, you may have a reason to sell the holding.

In essence, this is a code of discipline that professional portfolio managers use. They know why they own what they own as well as what they're worried about for any given company. When you own individual stocks, you're a portfolio manager, and like all good portfolio managers, you've got to find the right balance between conviction and uncertainty.

Action Steps

- Be sure your asset allocation is consistent with your goals and time horizon.
- Set realistic expectations for the performance of your overall portfolio.
- Make sure an individual fund's performance is consistent with its market segment and with your goals for the assets invested in it.
- For an actively managed fund, start with the fund's annual report for an assessment of strategy and performance.
- Write down your sources of conviction—and concern—for the individual stocks in your portfolio.

chapter eight

KEEP YOUR COSTS LOW

The costs of investing can create a wide gulf between the returns produced by the financial markets and the returns ultimately earned by investors. Some costs are unavoidable, but most of the "What Works" investors took steps to keep them to a reasonable minimum. After all, it's not how much you make, it's how much you keep.

Over an investing lifetime, the difference between high costs and low costs can be the difference between reaching your goals and coming up short. In this chapter, the "What Works" investors offer insight and advice on minimizing the costs imposed by the financial services industry. The next chapter takes up the most important derivative cost of investing: taxes. Together, investment costs and taxes are a one-two punch that can do a lot of damage to your portfolio.

Over an investing lifetime, the difference between high costs and low costs can be the difference between reaching your goals and coming up short.

Costs of Investing

All investment management firms charge money to provide investment services. They need to pay salaries, develop recordkeeping systems, buy or lease office space, and meet all the expenses of doing business. They also need to generate profits for the owners of the firm. Some firms may be owned by a group of partners or executives; others are owned by public shareholders. In recent years, many investment management firms have been acquired by large corporate owners, such as multinational banks. (The Vanguard Group is owned by the mutual funds—and indirectly the mutual fund shareholders—that it manages and administers, and returns its profits to shareholders in the form of lower expenses). Investment management companies cover most of their operating costs, and generate profits for their owners, through sales charges and asset-based fees.

Sales Charges

The "What Works" investors reserved their strongest objections for sales charges—the loads levied by mutual funds or the commissions charged on stock transactions. That's not surprising. These charges are the most visible, and as shareholders in the world's largest pure no-load mutual fund company, the "What Works" investors have, in effect, already declared their allegiance to no-load, low-cost investing.

> "I bought a fund from a broker some time ago for $10,000 and did not realize that I lost $800 in commissions the moment I signed it."

> "I don't want them to take anything out up front. When I invest $1,000 in a fund, I want $1,000 to go to work for me, and not have $200 or $300 taken out for fees."

> "I had a disappointing experience with high-cost 'experts' who were only brokers peddling high-load/high-commission products chasing hot sectors."

> "I've never purchased a load fund. There are very few advisers skilled enough to beat the averages, and my chances of picking them are slender."

> "My most disappointing experience was selling during the crash of the market in 1987. In hindsight, I should have ridden the downside out and taken a much longer-term view. The second most disappointing experience was getting involved in load funds early on. They sure didn't provide much performance for the money they charged."

There are many complicated variations of loads (back-end loads, level loads), but the traditional front-end load is much like the commission charged by a brokerage, with an important difference. A commission might be a flat fee of $40 a trade, but loads are assessed as a percentage of your initial investment. Both charges are taken out up front, but with loads, the more you invest, the more you pay—within limits. (Some loaded funds reduce their sales charges at different break points. You might pay a load of 5% on investments of less than $100,000, but only 3.75% on investments of more than $100,000, and perhaps no load on investments of $1 million or more.)

Load math is straightforward: If you invest $10,000 in a fund with a load of 6%, $9,400 of your money will go to work in the fund. The other $600 winds up with the fund company and the person who sells the fund. The load is meant to compensate the broker or adviser for his or her advice.

A common alternative to sales loads is 12b-1 fees (marketing fees). These charges are built into a fund's ongoing expenses. Each year the fund deducts as much as 1% of your assets (the regulatory limit) to pay the professional who sold you the fund and/or to market the fund to new investors. Over time, 12b-1 fees can cost far more than sales loads. The "What Works" investors took pains to avoid them, too.

Asset-Based Fees

Charges that aren't paid through initial sales charges are generally covered by asset-based fees, or ongoing charges assessed as a percentage of your assets. These fees were scarce in the brokerage industry until recently, but now some brokerages have replaced traditional commissions with a flat annual fee of, say, 1% or 2% of assets.

The most common asset-based fees are mutual fund expense ratios. (The expense ratio also includes the 12b-1 marketing fees, just discussed.) A mutual fund is an investment company (its legal name, and a good description of its actual activities). Just as operating companies such as General Motors or IBM must meet the costs of doing business, so must an investment company. It employs people to invest your money, maintain your account records, and provide administrative services on behalf of the fund. These costs are reported as an expense ratio (annual operating costs as a percentage of average net assets). If it costs $5 million a year to operate a fund with $500 million in assets, the fund has an expense ratio ($5 million/$500 million) of 1%.

The upper range of expense ratios is about 3.00% (a few fringe funds with legal troubles or oddball strategies and virtually no assets sport double-digit expense ratios), and the lower range is 0.12% to 0.20% for broad-based, passively managed index funds. The returns reported by mutual funds are always net of expenses. Perhaps because you can't see your money disappear, as you would with a sales charge, expense ratios can be easy to ignore. After all, these fees are not deducted on your statement. You never receive a bill. The charges come directly out of fund assets, before fund returns are reported. But as our investors explained, the expense ratio is real money.

> "Stay away from high expenses. Most likely, they're the ones making the money—not you."

> "Purchase funds that are free of loads and high management expenses."

> "I learned that it's a fool's goal to try to beat the market by a significant degree. I've learned that diversification, low cost, and dollar-cost averaging are extremely important investment goals."

> "[A big mistake is that] people do not do research. They take hot tips and buy. Try to time the market—in and out. They don't worry about loads and expenses."

> "Unsuccessful investors have a poor asset allocation. They try to pick individual stocks. They don't watch fees that are charged. Mistakes are made when they don't pay attention, even in a minimal way, to their accounts."

Transaction Costs

Other costs are harder to identify but can nevertheless be significant. Transaction costs are one example. When a mutual fund (or an individual) trades securities, it pays brokerage commissions, bid–ask spreads, and market-impact costs (the cost incurred when a large securities transaction causes the price to move, making the security more expensive to buy or less rewarding to sell). Your mutual fund's reported returns are net of transaction costs, so it's hard to figure out how much your fund is paying to transact in the markets. But clearly the more a fund trades, the higher its transaction costs.

In a 1997 *Journal of Finance* article, Mark C. Carhart estimated that a stock fund with annual turnover equal to 100% (about half of all stock funds trade more, half less) would incur total transaction costs of 0.95% a year.[1] (The turnover rate is a measure of a fund's trading activity. A turnover rate of 100% means that, during a year, a fund has bought or sold securities with a value equal to 100% of its average net assets.) Funds that trade half as much would incur costs half as large, and funds that trade twice as much would incur costs twice as large.

Our investors didn't say much about these relatively obscure costs, but a few did, and they took steps to minimize transaction costs.

> "Over the years (since 1980), I have become a believer in index investing in a low-fee index [fund], such as the Vanguard 500 Index. For three reasons: Broad market average, low turnover equals low commissions and taxes, and low management fees."

Miscellaneous Costs

Other fees and charges include account maintenance fees for accounts with low balances, account transfer fees, account inactivity fees at some brokerages, and on and on. Most of these are modest, but over time, the nickels and dimes can add up. Also, even if you invest in no-load mutual funds, it's important to remember that if you rely on the counsel of an adviser, you'll incur costs on top of those levied by the mutual fund in the form of asset-based or hourly fees. If professional advice can help you stay committed to a plan, however, these fees may be a bargain relative to the opportunity costs of ill-considered investment decisions.

Impact of Costs

How much do costs matter? As reported in Chapter 3 (Table 3.2), the investors we surveyed said "low costs" were the most important reason to select an investment management company. In fact, respondents rated "low costs" 11 percentage points more important than the next most highly rated attribute, "excellent customer service." High-net-worth investors, who can presumably afford to pay less attention to costs, actually pay more attention to costs than core investors. Perhaps their greater attention to costs reflected their greater investment experience (60% of high-net-worth investors described themselves as "experienced" or "highly experienced investors," while only 38% of core respondents did so). Both groups consider "low costs" significantly more important than "superior fund performance," the seemingly obvious reason to select an investment services provider.

Costs can be predicted with relative certainty, and as the investors noted earlier, investment performance is often fleeting and unpredictable. By selecting low-cost investments, you stack the odds in your favor. In a study published in 2002, investment research firm Morningstar ranked U.S. stock mutual funds by their 1996 expense ratios and then examined their returns over the five years ended December 2001.

"In short, we attempted to put ourselves in the shoes of an investor seeking to buy a stock fund five years ago to answer the following: Do investors who fish in the low-cost pond tend to earn better returns?"[2]

The data responded with a resounding yes. In eight of Morningstar's nine stock-fund categories, the funds with the lowest costs outperformed those with the highest (the exception was small-blend funds). The role of costs was so important, in fact, that the study came to this counterintuitive conclusion: "In most categories, investors would have been better off avoiding strong-performing, high-cost funds and instead picking a low-cost fund with a weak performance record"[3]—a conclusion that validates the "What Works" investors' cost-conscious approach to selecting an investment management company.

Over time, the cumulative impact of cost can be enormous. Consider two hypothetical $10,000 investments, one in a low-cost stock index fund tracking the broad stock market, and the other in the average actively managed stock fund (Figure 8.1). Both investments were held for the 20 years ended December 31, 2001. At the end of 2001, the index fund carried an annual expense ratio of 0.18%; the average actively managed fund charged 1.64%. After costs, the index fund returned an annualized 15.0% per year, while the average equity fund returned 13.0% (the average fund result would most likely have returned even less if many of the funds with the worst records had not gone out of business and disappeared from the historical databases).

As shown in Figure 8.1, at the end of the period, the index fund investor would have $163,665. In the average equity fund, that same $10,000 investment would have grown to just $115,231. (This figure excludes the impact of loads paid by many investors in actively managed funds.) Even a difference of 2 percentage points compounds to serious money over 20 years: $48,434. The average fund's shortfall relative to the index fund wound up in the pockets of the fund managers, traders, and administrators handling the account.

Of course, when the stock market is generating double-digit returns year in, year out, it's easy to shrug off a percentage point or two in fees

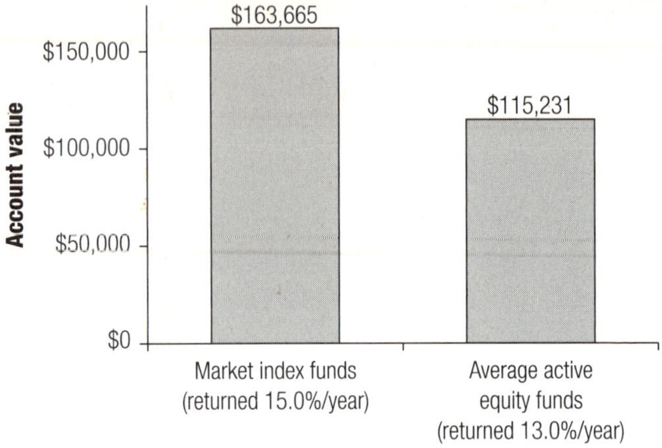

FIGURE 8.1 Growth of $10,000: 1981–2001.
Sources: The Vanguard Group, Inc.; mutual fund data from Lipper Inc.

(even if it means tens of thousands of dollars over a long time horizon). But high costs are harder to accept when returns grow lean. Say the market's return pulls back to 5% or so for an extended period. Suddenly, annual fees of 2% represent a full 40% of the market's bounty. "Costs are something I've kind of looked at in the past few years. It's more important now in this environment. When returns were very strong, there was more of a buffer for the costs," said a Boston attorney in his early thirties.

These stark mathematics have long been especially clear in asset classes such as bonds and money market funds, which have generated more modest long-term returns than stocks. "Cost wasn't important at first, but it is now. It's a big factor now, especially on the bonds. When they got this 'Yippee, here we go!' attitude, like we had in the 1990s, you didn't really think about costs," a retired investor from Texas told us. "I would say in the last four years—I guess when I turned just a bit beyond 70—that's when we started to think about cost."

Checking Prices in the Prospectus

A mutual fund's prospectus presents a clear picture of the fees you pay to invest in that fund. This information is useful when comparing the cost of different funds. Table 8.1 presents the fees charged by two S&P 500 Index–based mutual funds. The investment portfolios are identical, but the fees—and thus the potential returns earned by shareholders—will be very different. All data come from the funds' prospectuses.

Table 8.2 shows the dollar amounts you'd pay over time in each fund. The examples assume an initial investment of $10,000 and annual investment returns of 5%, per regulatory requirements.

TABLE 8.1 Comparing Fees Charged by Two S&P 500 Index Funds

	Fund A (%)	*Fund B (%)*
Maximum sales charge (load) imposed on purchases (as a percentage of offering price)	5.75	None
Management fees	0.25	0.16
Distribution (12b-1) fees	0	0
Other expenses	0.63	0.02
Total annual fund operating expenses	0.88	0.18
Fee waivers	0.21	0
Net expenses	0.67	0.18

Sources: Data from prospectuses dated February 1, 2002, for Wells Fargo Equity Index Fund Class A (Fund *A* in the example) and April 26, 2002, for Vanguard® 500 Index Fund Investor Shares (Fund *B*).

TABLE 8.2 Cumulative Cost of Investing Over Time in Fund A and Fund B

	1 Year	*3 Years*	*5 Years*	*10 Years*
Fund A	$640	$820	$1,015	$1,579
Fund B	18	58	101	230

Notes: Data on expenses are based on a $10,000 investment in each fund and assume a 5% annual return in each. For identification of Funds *A* and *B*, see sources to Table 8.1.

'Cutting Costs to the Bone'

The "What Works" investors offered a number of suggestions for keeping costs low. "Buy no-load funds with low expense ratios" and "use discount brokerages" were frequent words to the wise. Several investors also urged people to "understand their costs," which might seem obvious, except that costs can be surprisingly complicated. One woman said her most disappointing experience was "going to a discount broker who ended up expensive, and I am more or less stuck with them. Too many fees, even transfer fees, which prevent me from moving out." Respondents also advised investors to consider index funds, which are among the lowest-cost investment vehicles.

> "Start as soon as possible and invest as much as is possible and allowed. Invest in low-cost, well-managed mutual funds."

> "Stick to index stock funds and low costs."

> "Research, research, research. Then choose an honest, low-cost entity to facilitate your decisions."

> "Choosing quality and economical management are of great importance."

> "Be analytical. Be patient. Go with a reputable investment firm. Consider the cost of your investments and pick low-cost funds and discount brokerages. Save early and consistently."

> "Save regularly, especially via tax-sheltered programs. Have a long-term asset-allocation plan and stick to it. Emphasize low-cost index funds as core holdings of the portfolio."

> "The biggest mistake investors make is thinking they, or their financial adviser, can pick winning stocks. Because they don't understand how difficult it is to beat the market, net of all costs."

"I think over the long haul, low costs make all the difference over having some flash-in-the-pan manager. Get the most you reasonably can for the least."

"Ask lots of questions. Know the fees involved in transactions. Do lots of research. Learn the basics of investment."

"I like commonsense advice: Keep expenses low, don't try to get rich overnight, and invest for the long term."

"Cut investment costs to the bone."

Costs can have a big impact on your success as an investor. Fortunately, they're easy to control. Whatever your investment goals, you can find a low-cost portfolio to help you implement your plan. And the research—and experience—is clear: Lower costs lead to higher returns. Unlike the financial markets' returns, which are impossible to predict, costs hold pretty steady. High-cost investment options tend to stay expensive, and low-cost alternatives tend to stay inexpensive.

In the next chapter, the "What Works" investors give us the lowdown on a sizable cost that, sooner or later, affects almost every portfolio: taxes. Just as you can take simple steps to minimize the impact of investment costs, it's relatively easy to limit the tax collector's participation in your portfolio. Sensible tax management can hasten your progress toward your goals. But beware: As many of our investors have learned, excessive attention to tax reduction can warp your investment plan. That is, you may wind up with investments that not only generate little in the way of taxes but, more important, little in the way of returns.

The Critical Connection: Low Cost Equals High Value

by Francis M. Kinniry Jr.

Francis M. Kinniry Jr., a principal in Vanguard's Investment Counseling & Research group, sets the investment policy and methodology used by Vanguard's advisory services, including those for high-net-worth clients. He also directs comprehensive wealth management for a select group of investors. Mr. Kinniry, who joined Vanguard in 1997, is a Chartered Financial Analyst.

"What Works" investors make a connection between low cost and investment success that too many people miss. Low costs aren't an end in themselves; the important thing is what low costs lead to: higher returns.

A few years ago, we did a study for clients of Vanguard's Asset Management and Trust Services to determine the most important predictors of future mutual fund performance. We looked at an exhaustive array of statistics—R-squared, style purity, the information ratio (a relative measure of return and risk), and so on. The most important predictor of future performance, by far, was cost. Reducing your costs is the most reliable way to earn higher returns.

Academic research indicates that the best institutional investment managers outperform the stock market by 50 to 80 basis points (0.50–0.80 percentage point) or so per year before costs. In our highly competitive financial markets, that's extraordinary—the kind of talent that commands high fees in almost all fields of endeavor. But after deducting their costs—management fees, transaction costs, the drag of holding cash—research also shows that these skilled managers give up their advantage and wind up behind the broad market.

The Investing Paradox

Most people don't equate low cost with high value, because in most economic decisions, we're conditioned to see the opposite. You can tell the difference between a $300 suit and a $100 suit when you put it on. If you need an operation, you're not going to shop for the low-cost doctor. People worry that in pursuing lower-cost investments, they'll be putting their nest egg in the equivalent of a $100 suit or entrusting it to an ill-trained surgeon. And high-cost investment providers prey on these fears. But the "What Works" investors know that when you say, "I want the highest-quality investment services" or the "highest total return," what you're really saying is, "I want to keep my costs as low as reasonably possible."

Some "What Works" investors advocated index funds for low-cost investing. I'd add that a distinction more critical than that between indexing and active management is the distinction between low costs and high costs. If you invest in index funds, low costs enhance your ability to match the index's returns. It makes no sense to invest in a high-cost index fund. You can also invest with a world-class active manager at a very modest expense ratio of 40 or 50 basis points. At that level, costs aren't going to be a significant detractor from any excess returns these talented managers *may* produce. Sophisticated institutional investors, such as pension funds, endowments, and foundations, understand the critical nature of costs, so they negotiate aggressively to get low management fees from the investment managers they hire.

Action Steps

- Once you select a mix of asset classes and choose an investment strategy (such as active or passive management), try to maximize your investments' returns by minimizing their costs. In investment management, the traditional economic relationship between higher costs and higher quality is turned on its head. You don't sacrifice anything by paying less; you get more.
- Beware of the persuasive—but wrong—pitch from high-cost investment providers who warn that "you get what you pay for." That may be true if you're shopping for a car, but the reverse is true in investments.
- Pay attention to *all* costs: expense ratios or management fees, transaction costs, taxes, commissions, tracking error, and any miscellaneous fees. Your goal is to minimize your *all-in* costs. After all, if an index fund boasts low management fees, but is unable to replicate the returns of its benchmark or incurs significant transaction costs, your all-in costs may be high.

chapter nine

BE SMART ABOUT TAXES

Smart tax management can be a powerful contributor to the success of your investment plan. According to data from investment research firm Morningstar, taxes trimmed the return of the average stock fund by 2.5 percentage points a year during the 1990s—more than was consumed by mutual fund operating and transaction costs. Just as limiting fund costs hastens your progress toward your financial goals, reducing the tax collector's take enhances your prospects of success.

The "What Works" investors offered several suggestions for managing taxes on your investments. They're strong advocates of tax-deferred investing through employer-sponsored retirement plans and IRAs. They also explained how you can minimize the tax collector's participation in your taxable portfolio by investing in tax-efficient vehicles and keeping trading to a minimum. Although the principles presented in this chapter are timeless, the specific strategies are not. The tax code is always in flux. At the start of 2003, for example, President George W. Bush proposed dramatic changes to the taxation of stock dividends and to the features of various tax-advantaged savings accounts. At the moment, however, these proposals are just proposals. This chapter addresses the tax law that existed as *Wealth of Experience* was being written.

Survey respondents supplemented their advice with another valuable tool, one often lost in the effort to cut taxes: perspective. They urged investors not to be lured by schemes designed solely to trim their tax bill.

Many of them learned this lesson the hard way in tax shelters such as real estate or oil and gas partnerships. After all, your goal is not to reduce taxes; it's to maximize your after-tax returns. "Make good investments and give the government its due," said one investor. Fortunately, the goals of sound investing and smart tax management rarely conflict.

How Your Investments Are Taxed

Investment returns come in the form of capital gains or income. Both are subject to federal and (depending on where you live) state taxes, though the rates and the timing can differ. Federal income tax rates run as high as 38.6%, depending on your overall income and marital filing status. Realized capital gains on investments held for less than one year are taxed at income tax rates. For investments held more than a year, the rates peak at 20% (10% for investors in the lowest tax bracket).

You generally owe taxes when:

- You receive a dividend payment from a stock or mutual fund or an interest payment from a bond or bank account.
- You sell a security (stock, bond, mutual fund share) for more than your purchase price, thus realizing a capital gain.
- You receive a capital gain distribution from a mutual fund. (When a mutual fund trades securities at a profit, it must distribute that profit to fund shareholders.)

There are notable exceptions to these guidelines:

- U.S. Treasury securities, whose interest income is subject to federal income tax, but exempt from state taxes.
- Municipal bonds (muni bonds), whose interest income is not only exempt from federal income tax but may also be exempt from state income taxes and in some instances, local income taxes.

If you hold mutual funds in a taxable account, you must pay taxes on dividend and capital gains distributions, even if you reinvest those distributions in the fund. A mutual fund can distribute a taxable gain even if the fund declines in value. Some investors find this particularly irksome. One "What Works" respondent said her most disappointing investment experience was "getting hit with $8,000 capital gains tax on a losing mutual fund."

Tax-Advantaged Investing: Retirement Accounts

Individual retirement accounts and employer-sponsored retirement plans, such as 401(k) and 403(b) plans, are two of the most effective vehicles for enhancing your after-tax returns. (The tax treatment of investments in tax-deferred annuities is somewhat similar, but these insurance-related products are beyond the scope of this chapter. Annuities weren't significant holdings among the "What Works" respondents.) IRAs and employer-sponsored plans receive similar tax treatment. Contributions are made with pre-tax dollars, which trim your current tax bill by reducing your taxable income. These accounts allow you to defer taxes on your investments and any earnings until you withdraw the money. Contributions to a Roth IRA, a relatively recent variation on the traditional IRA, are made with after-tax dollars, but your investment earnings are never taxed. (Internal Revenue Service rules on eligibility for these accounts change annually. Consult an investment company or the IRS to find out which accounts are right for you.)

The "What Works" investors were especially keen on employer-sponsored plans, not only for their tax benefits but also for the painless savings discipline they impose on participants. Contributions are deducted from your paycheck and invested before you have a chance to think about (or spend) the money. Many employers supplement their employees' savings, too, contributing perhaps $0.50 for every dollar saved. Life doesn't present many opportunities to turn $1.00 into $1.50 in the time it takes your payroll department to wire your savings to the investment manager.

> "Max out all your tax-deferred options, such as a 401(k) plan. Fund a Roth IRA every year. Do you really need a new car?"

> "I did not have a goal; I just wanted to invest in pre-tax money to lower my taxes."

> "Save a minimum of 15% of your gross pay for investments and maximize your employer's contribution for any 401(k) plans."

> One investor called his decision "to set up and participate in a tax-deferred savings plan in a professional corporation" his biggest investment success.

> "Deferring income into a tax-deferred account was my best experience," one investor said. "The lesson is in the value of compounding and how that really set me up to retire at 55."

As Figure 9.1 shows, tax deferral is like rocket fuel for the awesome engine of compounding. The figure assumes two hypothetical investments of $1, each generating a pre-tax return of 7% a year. The earnings on one investment are taxed every year, while taxes due on the other investment are deferred for 25 years and then subjected to the highest income tax rate.

The $1 invested in a tax-deferred account is actually equivalent to 61.4 cents invested in a taxable account (for investors with a marginal tax rate of 38.6%). The tax-deferred $1 will be subject to income taxes when it is eventually withdrawn. In a taxable account, the $1 is taxed before it's invested.

At the end of 25 years, the investment that is nicked year after year by the tax collector is worth $1.76. (Again, an after-tax investment of $1

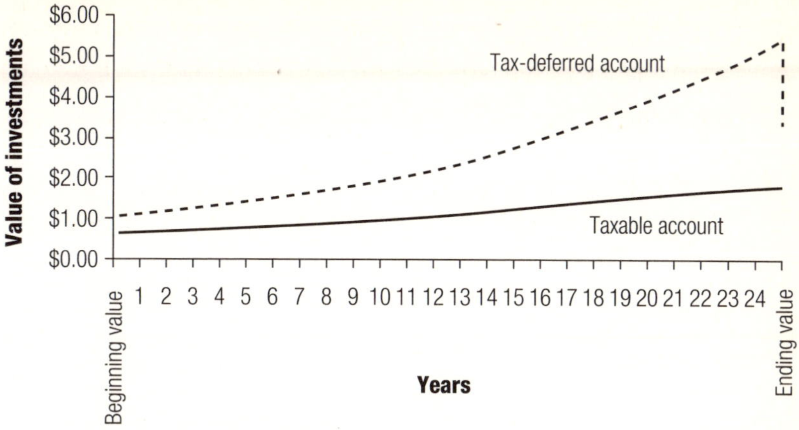

FIGURE 9.1 Advantage of tax deferral.

Source: The Vanguard Group, Inc.

Note: Figure assumes each hypothetical investment returns 7% a year, before taxes.

is equivalent to a pre-tax investment of 61.4 cents.) Before the final reckoning with the tax collector, the tax-deferred $1 is worth $5.43. After the federal government takes its 38.6% share, the investment is worth $3.33, still significantly more than the investment that was taxed every year. And the longer you defer taxes, the greater the reward for doing so.

There's a good reason the "What Works" investors were so enthusiastic about Roth IRAs. Contributions to a Roth IRA don't reduce your current taxable income, but your investment earnings can grow tax-free forever. Figure 9.2 shows hypothetical investments of $1 in both a Roth IRA and a taxable account. (Both contributions are after-tax, so $1 invested in a Roth is equivalent to $1 invested in the taxable account.) Both investments earn 7% a year, before taxes. After 25 years, the Roth investment is worth $5.43, while the taxable dollar is worth $2.86. Roth IRAs can be especially valuable to young investors, whose long time horizons allow them to derive the greatest benefit from the power of tax-free compounding.

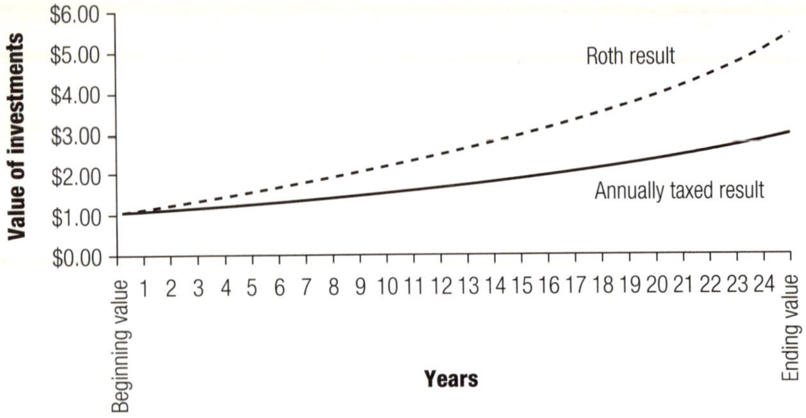

FIGURE 9.2 Advantage of tax-free growth in Roth IRA.

Source: The Vanguard Group, Inc.

Note: Figure assumes each hypothetical investment returns 7% a year before taxes.

"My wife and I don't have children, but three years ago, we started giving each of our nieces/nephews monies each year to fund Roth IRAs. They have had to endure a bit of a lecture on the value of an investment program (and Roth IRAs in particular), but I think they have appreciated our effort and have learned from it."

"My two children have had savings accounts since they were old enough to earn money. I would match their babysitting and lawn-mowing money, which would go into the bank, and later, I would contribute an amount equal to their earned income (usually $400) to a Roth IRA."

IRA Eligibility and Contribution Limits

Table 9.1 shows the maximum amounts you may contribute to your IRA (whether Roth or traditional) from 2003 through 2008. Investors aged 50 and over can contribute more than younger investors.

You're eligible to contribute to a traditional IRA if:

- You won't reach age 70½ in the current year.
- Your earned income is at least equal to your contribution. Your income level affects the deductibility of your contributions.

You're eligible to contribute to a Roth IRA if your income level is less than the limits set by the U.S. Treasury, which change annually. If you're eligible, your earned income must at least equal your contribution.

TABLE 9.1 IRA Maximum Annual Contribution: 2003–2008

Year	*Maximum contribution (under age 50)*[a]	*Maximum contribution (aged 50 and over)*[b]
2003	$3,000	$3,500
2004	3,000	3,500
2005	4,000	4,500
2006	4,000	5,000
2007	4,000	5,000
2008	5,000	6,000

Source: The Vanguard Group, Inc.

[a]If you're married and filing jointly, a contribution may be made on behalf of a nonworking spouse. The total contribution for you and your spouse cannot exceed the income of the working spouse in the year of the contribution.

[b]For individuals aged 50 and over as of the end of a tax year.

Note: After 2008, the annual IRA contribution limit will be indexed for inflation in $500 increments.

Tax-Advantaged Investing: Tax-Efficient Funds

Tax-efficient funds are a means of enhancing your after-tax returns within a taxable account. Some funds make tax minimization an explicit objective. Others employ strategies that are inherently tax efficient. Tax-efficient vehicles include stock index funds, tax-managed funds (often indexlike funds), and municipal bond funds.

- Stock index funds, especially those tracking broad market indexes, are generally tax efficient because they simply buy and hold the stocks in an index. The result is modest portfolio turnover, and thus a low level of realized capital gains that must be distributed to shareholders. The same logic suggests that it pays to limit your own trading, whether you invest in mutual funds or individual securities. A Texas investor who has managed his own portfolio since the 1970s said a common mistake was "investing in too many different mutual funds and then transferring amounts between different funds, only to end up with a large tax bill."
- Advisers of tax-managed funds use a variety of techniques, such as avoiding stocks that pay high dividends (taxable at investors' generally higher income tax rates) and offsetting realized gains with realized losses. Some funds also levy redemption fees to discourage shareholders from short-term trading, which can compromise a fund's tax-management strategies.
- Tax-exempt bond funds, also known as municipal or "muni" funds, generate income that is exempt from federal income tax, and in some cases, from state and local tax. Because of their tax exemption, these funds generally provide a lower yield than taxable bonds of similar maturity and quality. To compare a muni fund's yield with that of a taxable bond fund, you need to calculate its taxable-equivalent yield. This figure is equal to the muni fund's yield divided by 1 minus your income tax rate. If the muni fund yields 4.5%, and you're in the 38.6% tax bracket, you divide 4.5% by 1 minus 0.386. The result is a taxable-equivalent yield of 7.3%.

Where to Hold What

Your after-tax returns are affected by both the form of your investment return (income, capital gains, or both) and the tax treatment of your account (tax-advantaged or taxable). You can enhance your returns by keeping the right investments in the right accounts. For example, it doesn't make sense to hold a tax-exempt municipal bond fund in an IRA. The fund's income is already exempt from federal taxes, and there's no benefit to collecting it in a tax-deferred wrapper. In fact, there are big disadvantages. When you withdraw muni-bond earnings from a traditional IRA, the withdrawals are taxed at regular income tax rates. By using the wrong account, an investor transforms tax-free income into taxable income.

Some "What Works" investors discussed both the value of keeping the right investments in the right accounts and the cost of not doing so. Others related how the interplay between investment returns and account types informed their selling and rebalancing decisions.

> "This is counterintuitive, but it may be better to buy bonds in a nontaxable account and hold stocks in a taxable account. The 20% capital gains [rate] for stock is much better than the 30% to 40% tax on ordinary bond income."

> A Pennsylvania woman lamented that she hadn't undertaken a similar analysis before investing. "We made a lot of mistakes, the biggest being that we're paying so much in income taxes." She and her husband hold in a taxable account a bond-heavy balanced fund that generated relatively high levels of investment income. "We've paid taxes on all the income over the years," she said.

> "We look at my IRA, my wife's IRA, and our trust account as one fund. If there's any maneuvering or selling, we do it in the tax-deferred accounts so we don't have to pay the taxes." This

investor anticipated some portfolio adjustments as he and his wife prepared to sell their home and move into a retirement community. By conducting these transactions with an eye on tax efficiency, the couple will retain more resources to pay for their needs.

Tax-Smart Selling

If you need to raise cash for a purchase, maneuvering within a tax-deferred account isn't much help. "I purchased a new home and used money from shares of funds toward the down payment. I then had to pay capital gains taxes on the withdrawals," wrote a 40-year-old from Pennsylvania who has invested for about a decade. "I should have considered obtaining the initial funds for the home from another source to eliminate the tax consequences." One possibility might have been to sell shares on which he had a loss or the smallest gain.

Unfortunately, it's usually not that simple. When deciding what to sell, you need to consider not only the investment's return prospects but also the tax implications of a sale. If you believe that an investment boasts exceptional prospects, selling is foolish, even if doing so makes tax sense. On the other hand, if the investment's prospects are dim, it's wise to sell and lock in a gain, despite the tax consequences. That said, making accurate judgments about an investment's future is easier said than done.

> "Our most disappointing investment has been in the shares of Norfolk Southern Corp., which we have held since the 1970s (my wife worked for the predecessor, Southern Railway). In the 1990s, the company overpaid for the acquisition of Conrail and funded it with debt. The company has been forced to cut the dividend, and the share price has dropped. The lesson to be learned is to sell a company's shares when it becomes evident that management has blundered, even though the income taxes on the sale will be substantial."

"I've invested with [major mutual fund company] for several years and have made significant returns. I did not sell when I should have, and now have lost significant portions of my investment. Unfortunately, I will need some of this money soon. On the positive side, taking the loss should offset other potential gains for tax purposes."

"I was too concerned with taxes. I failed to sell real estate and stocks, even though I realized that they were overpriced."

Taxes Are Just One Consideration

The "What Works" investors recounted a number of other experiences that illustrate the danger of focusing on tax reduction to the exclusion of investment considerations. Good tax management is good investment management. As the "What Works" investors have learned, you can accomplish both objectives with a low-cost buy-and-hold strategy. People who pursue "investment" opportunities with the sole aim of trimming their tax bills often wind up regretting it.

"Back during my years of high earnings, we were proselytized by some tax advisers to go into some things like cattle and tugboats and bull sperm. All those things turned out to be catastrophes because they were declared illegal, and we wound up having to pay back taxes and penalties and so forth. Brahma bulls—they were going to breed them and raise them and sell them all over the world. You'd profit from the offspring. It turned out that they wound up selling more Brahma bulls than there were in the world. I think the fellow who started it wound up in jail. The adviser's pitch was that no matter what your income, you wouldn't have to pay any income tax. Any normal person would realize that this was not going to fly, but the financial adviser gave a good presentation. A number of us were hoodwinked. At that time, there was an almost confiscatory level of taxation. So anything you could do to reduce taxes seemed smart."

Before 1986, oddball tax shelters were commonplace, a reflection of the era's tax code. "This was that strange period when people were investing in art," one investor told us. "I bought a Rembrandt print." With federal tax reform in 1986, marginal tax rates dropped sharply, and the U.S. Congress closed the loopholes that had made these vehicles attractive. Once they lost their tax benefits, the vehicles had to stand on their investment merits. They collapsed.

> "I wanted to invest in real estate, but my wife didn't want to. Her family had owned some apartment buildings near the shipyards, and she wanted nothing to do with being a landlord. This fellow got me involved with a limited partnership, and I thought 'Okay, this is a path to real estate.' This involved everything from raw land up in Tacoma to a REIT [real estate investment trust]. He had most of my money, and invested it in various limited partnerships. He even convinced me to borrow against my insurance policy to invest in real estate. I didn't realize until too late that this was not the place to be. You had no way to sell those things; they were illiquid investments. And to have most of your investments in illiquid assets is goofy. These were heavy-duty tax shelters. And then Congress screwed it up in 1986, and the limited partnerships went to hell."

> "Real estate tax shelters in the 1980s had no economic value, other than the tax deductions, which virtually evaporated when the tax laws were changed in 1986."

Advice on Tax-Smart Investing

Even as the tax code has again increased in complexity in recent years, investments with economic value have been a prerequisite for earning strong after-tax returns. A vehicle that can produce little in the way of real earnings and income and instead seeks to cash in on quirks in the tax code is forever at risk of change in the political winds. In the past, our investors dabbled in exotic schemes that promised big tax savings, and for the most part, they lost. (Although many of these shelters have disappeared, there will always be new ones to take their place. Whenever there are taxes to be avoided, there are tax shelters to be created. Whether they hold up to regulatory scrutiny is always a risk.) Today, these investors favor tax-efficient funds and tax-advantaged accounts that keep investment in the driver's seat, with a tax-reducing kicker.

> "Take advantage of any 401(k), 403(b), or other tax-deferred savings. Don't listen to your buddies. Their investment advice ranks with fishermen describing the size of their catch."

> "Save regularly in tax-deferred vehicles, using index funds as basic investments."

> "Be aware of funds that have low stock turnover with consequently low tax liability in most cases."

> "Invest in tax-deferred accounts, start early, and invest the greatest amount possible."

> "My most disappointing experience was investing in real estate limited partnerships to minimize current income taxes. I learned to avoid schemes that tout the savings as a principal objective."

> "Save 20% of after-tax income in some form. Maximize 401(k) matches. Watch out for taxes. Diversify."

> A costly mistake is "taking money out of IRA/401(k)-type accounts. Young people don't appreciate the value of time and of tax-deferred money. In a *major* crisis, take out what is needed. But know what advantages you are giving up."

"(1) Save regularly, especially via tax-sheltered programs.
(2) Have a long-term asset allocation plan and stick to it.
(3) Emphasize low-cost index funds as core holdings of the portfolio."

The investors' advice to keep an eye on investment costs and taxes aims to help you defend your assets against a potentially devastating one-two combination. By minimizing costs and taking steps to maximize after-tax returns, you enhance your chances of going the distance to your financial goals.

In the next chapter, "What Works" investors discuss issues to consider when your long-term plans are securely on track and your goals are within sight: your legacy, both familial and financial.

Taxes: It's Not What You Pay, It's What You Keep

by Joel Dickson

Joel Dickson, a principal in Vanguard's Quantitative Equity Group, joined the company in 1996. As a doctoral candidate at Stanford University, Mr. Dickson was coauthor of a research paper that is still considered the seminal study on mutual fund tax efficiency.

Before coming to Vanguard, Mr. Dickson worked as a staff economist at the Federal Reserve Board. He has testified before the U.S. Congress on Social Security reform and mutual fund disclosure issues.

The experiences of the "What Works" investors suggest an important theme: It's not what you pay in taxes, it's what you keep after taxes. Many investors miss this. At Vanguard, we see too many people who, quite appropriately, hold municipal bonds while working, when their tax rates are high, but then continue to hold these investments in retirement, when their tax rates fall and muni bonds no longer generate higher after-tax returns than taxable bonds.

The same theme suggests that low-cost investments are more tax efficient than high-cost funds, even though they may produce a larger tax bill. Suppose you have two funds holding stocks with average dividend yields of 1.5% before costs. If the low-cost fund charges an expense ratio of 0.5% of assets per year, you receive a dividend of 1%, on which you pay taxes of 38.6% (for those in the highest income tax bracket). If the high-cost fund charges 1.5% of assets per year, you receive no income dividend and owe no taxes. But are you better off? You've effectively paid a 100% tax to the fund company with the high expense ratio. I'd rather pay 38.6 cents to the government and keep 61.4 cents than pay a 100% "tax" to the fund company.

Tax efficiency is a *maximization* issue, not a *minimization* issue. You want to *maximize* your after-tax returns, not *minimize* your taxes. Unfortunately, resistance to taxes can be so strong that some investors accept lower returns simply to avoid writing a check to the IRS. I would second the advice of the investor quoted earlier who said, "Make good investments and give the government its due."

Tax-Efficient Investment and Investors

A second theme pointed out by "What Works" investors is that tax-efficient investing requires not only tax-efficient *investments* but also tax-efficient *investors*. It's not sufficient to have one or the other. If you buy tax-efficient investments, but trade them every two years, you give up virtually all of the tax efficiency.

I was impressed by the comments of the investor who viewed his wife's and his IRAs and trust accounts as one big portfolio in which they can make any adjustments in a tax-efficient manner. That's the most productive approach, but it's also rare. More commonly we see people trade more frequently in taxable accounts than in their tax-advantaged accounts, such as IRAs and 401(k) plans. In the end, all these accounts are just one big portfolio to help meet your cash-flow needs in the future.

Shelters and Lessons

The "What Works" investors' bad experiences with investments sold more on their tax benefits than on their investment merits convey a very important lesson: The tax code is not static. The wealth we will realize in the future will depend on both the current tax system and the uncertain future tax system. Our future after-tax income will be influenced by factors such as whether or not Social Security benefits are taxed and the income and capital-gains tax rates on our investments. Can anyone possibly know what those rates will be 10 or 25 years in the future?

That's why the Roth IRA is so powerful: It provides *tax-code diversification.* Why do you invest in many different stocks and bonds? To limit your exposure to the risk of any one security. You can do the same thing on the tax side. Some of your accounts offer tax advantages today. A 401(k) plan, for example, allows you to deduct your contributions from your current income, so you save on taxes now. Those contributions and any earnings are taxed in the future, when the money is withdrawn. With a Roth IRA, you contribute after-tax dollars. You get no tax benefit today, but you get to make tax-free withdrawals of the contributions and any earnings in the future.

Many investors ask us, "Should I invest in a Roth IRA or in my employer's plan or traditional IRA?" For many investors, the answer is not either/or—it's that you should invest in all of them. Holding a Roth IRA in combination with one of the traditional retirement-savings vehicles provides a means of diversifying your exposure to potential changes in future tax laws.

Action Steps

- Pursue the highest after-tax returns, even if doing so means writing a larger check to the IRS. Smart tax management is a maximization issue, not a minimization issue.
- Tax-efficient investments are not enough; you also need to limit trading that would produce capital gains in taxable accounts. Conduct any such transactions in tax-advantaged accounts such as IRAs and 401(k) plans.
- Consider the Roth IRA as a tool for "tax-code diversification."

chapter ten
CREATE YOUR INVESTING LEGACY

As you grow older, you begin to think about investing beyond your own lifetime. If you're young, just starting in a tax-advantaged retirement plan, the next generation isn't yet a concern. But it will be. Even if you don't have dependents, and even if you don't intend to leave behind a financial estate, the influence of your investment practices may be felt long after your demise.

The bridge between your portfolio and future generations might be a financial bequest to your survivors or a charitable organization. This is the realm of estate planning. Or maybe your legacy is the lessons and habits you impart to your children and other family members.

The "What Works" investors have given the legacy issue considerable thought. Some of them have benefited from a previous generation's bequest of knowledge, money, or both, and many also believed it's important to provide the same head start to a new generation of investors.

This chapter reviews the "What Works" investors' insights on the role of families in shaping investment habits, as well as strategies used by some to encourage their family members to start saving and investing. Some approaches to teaching young people the habits of thrift and investing were striking in their originality and power—valuable tips for anyone hoping to inspire a new investor. Respondents also touch on issues to consider if a substantial charitable donation might be in your plans. And though this chapter isn't a how-to, it offers a review of estate-planning basics.

Intergenerational Goals

The most obvious intergenerational goals are to pay for children's or grandchildren's education and to leave an estate for your heirs. A relatively small percentage of the "What Works" investors have made these goals explicit objectives of their investment programs, as indicated in Table 10.1. Overall, 12% of respondents considered it very important to leave an estate for their heirs, and 10% said that investing for the education of children or grandchildren was extremely important to them. It may seem surprising that these goals didn't rank higher, but the median age of the "What Works" investors was 65, with only 30% younger than 60, perhaps beyond the age at which saving for education is an important goal, but not yet at an age when they're focusing on building a financial bequest for their heirs. It's also possible that in a world of limited resources, people simply focused on retirement. After all, bor-

TABLE 10.1 Intergenerational Goals (Percentage of 'What Works' respondents who said 'extremely important')

	Total (%)	*Core (%)*	*High-net-worth (%)*
Saving for retirement	47	57	45
General savings for the future	28	34	27
Avoid or reduce taxes	19	18	20
Current income	18	14	19
Building an estate to leave for heirs	12	12	13
Children's/grandchildren's education	10	14	9

Source: The Vanguard Group, Inc.

rowing to pay for college can be a smart "investment," but borrowing to pay for retirement is not really an option.

Indeed, a study conducted by the Investment Company Institute (ICI), a mutual fund trade group, reached similar findings. In 2001, the ICI reported that 72% of mutual fund investors said retirement was their primary investment objective; only 11% cited financing children's education as their primary objective.[1]

Many respondents told us, in addition, that bequests to charity were an important objective. A charitable gift provides obvious financial benefits to the recipient. A few investors noted that these gifts also produce substantial tax (as well as psychological) benefits for the giver. A gift reduces the size of your estate, thus reducing your heirs' potential estate-tax liability, and you can generally deduct your charitable gift from your income, thereby reducing your current income taxes.

Some investors noted that donating appreciated securities (stocks most typically, but also fund shares) can be an especially productive means of giving, as illustrated in Table 10.2. If you own securities with a market value of $10,000 and an unrealized gain of $8,000, you can donate securities without first selling and paying $1,600 in capital gains taxes. You get a tax deduction for the full $10,000, and the beneficiary gets a larger gift with which to pursue its good works. If the charity needs to sell your securities, it can do so without tax consequences.

TABLE 10.2 After-Tax Value of Two Gifts

	Gift of shares	*Gift of cash from the sale of shares*
Value of shares	$10,000	$10,000
Unrealized gain	8,000	8,000
Sales proceeds	N.A.	10,000
Tax liability	0	1,600
Gift value	10,000	8,400
Donor's deduction	10,000	8,400

Source: The Vanguard Group, Inc.

"My most successful experience was buying 250 shares of Anheuser-Busch stock in 1980 and just holding onto it. As I look back on this, it's my best example of real investing. I was not buying and selling stock; I was not moving it in and out of a position. I bought a good company and held it. It was an important component of the account my wife and I set up at [major independent public charity]."

"I should have donated more of my appreciated stocks to set up a charitable trust and thus given more to charity." With a little planning, this investor might have been able to boost his donations by as much as 20%.

"My goal was to make enough through work and investing to be able to retire early and live well, while at the same time increasing charitable giving."

Another investor aimed to "put children through college. Retire comfortably, and travel extensively in U.S. and around the world. Continue charitable work and giving."

"The biggest thought I have now is how am I going to use that money? I'm financially independent. I don't even need those investments. My concern is, if I sell some of the land I've got, where can I give the money so that it will do the most good?"

Passing Along Survival Skills

Even if they haven't yet included the next generation in their investment plans, many of these investors have encouraged their spouses, children, or friends to take an interest in investing. Their approaches, and their success, vary. Some people, for whatever reason, have no interest in acquiring what is tantamount to a survival skill in the modern economy. Others take to it with a zeal that surpasses that of their tutors.

"What Works" survey responses indicated that investment evangelizers most often preached to their children. Spouses were a smaller audience (perhaps because many couples were already partners in an investment program), and other family members and friends filled the remaining pews. These results square with what little independent research has been done on the role of the family in encouraging people to save and invest.

Parents, Youth & Money Survey, a 2001 survey by the Employee Benefit Research Institute (EBRI), identified parents as the primary teachers of money management.[2] That's not surprising. The subject isn't widely taught. As recently as a generation ago, the schools' approach to personal finance rarely extended beyond comparing the unit prices of cans of peas in home economics. That's useful, but it's not going to get you very far in the capital markets.

As you might expect, the higher a family's income, the more likely it is that the children will be exposed to different financial products and services. EBRI's survey found that among households with incomes of $75,000 or more, 82% of parents indicated that their child had a savings account. Among households with incomes of $35,000 or less, the figure was 57%. In the higher-income households, 30% of children had mutual fund accounts; in the lower-income households, the figure was just 7%.[3]

However, the strategies many parents shared with us really don't depend on access to a broad spectrum of products and services. Mostly they emphasized the simple act of saving and the financial and emotional benefits of postponing current consumption for a more valuable goal in the future.

Disciplined Saving and an IRA at Age 17

In investing, simple is usually more productive than complex. The same seems to hold true in teaching others to invest. Consider the success of this simple, commonsensical approach used by a Maryland mother of two.

"We set up an allowance for each of the boys. The money had to be broken up in three parts. One part could be spent right away, one part had to be saved for six weeks, and the last third had to be saved for long-term goals, such as college. As time went on, they started to say, 'I can save for a little longer than six weeks' for a bigger purchase." Although Laurel Murphy has been investing in mutual funds for more than 20 years, she has emphasized saving, rather than investing, with her children. "I think lessons on investing should come quite a bit farther down the road after lessons on saving and spending. I'm one of those first-things-first people. When my older son got into his eighth-grade math class, the math teacher decided to have everybody pick a stock as part of a math project. My son bought Netscape. Well, he won the prize for the class, because it was up over 1,000% that year. If he had had real money in there, I think he would have thought things always go up. I think it's much better to go slow at it and to have the first experiment about risk be small and work your way up, rather than plunging right away into P/E ratios and such."

Now that Ms. Murphy's older son is working, "I have matched his earnings in an IRA. He therefore pays no income taxes, and I made him figure out how much the account will be worth when he retires. It makes a huge impression! I will do it again for my younger son. (By the way, you should see the looks we get when a 17-year-old is making a deposit to his IRA.)"

"When my grandchildren get presents, I give a savings bond. When they graduate from high school, I give them a mutual fund. My purpose is to try to introduce some investment instruments into their lives. Of course, I put a few dollars in cash along with the gift. That lets them spend something right away."

"Investing is a must. Even my one-week-old to ten-year-old grandchildren own stocks."

"We obtained Social Security numbers for the kids when they were infants and started to buy individual stocks for them and encouraged grandparents to do the same. At first these stocks were going to be a college fund, but thanks to a double income, we didn't spend a dime of each kid's fund. Instead, we ended up signing over about $30,000 to each child when he was in his early 20s. Each kid is now a regular investor."

A grandmother told us that she began "investing in IRAs for my children and working grandchildren, hoping they would add to it. I also emphasized starting young and the 'Rule of 72,' where investments double every so many years."

"I scared my sister into investing by insisting she would not have enough money for retirement if she didn't."

"I bought the book *The Richest Man in Babylon* [a 1920s-era motivational book about saving and investing by George S. Clason] for many people. My sons have accumulated moderate holdings with no debt."

"We started educating our children about investing early, and they are starting their children even earlier. They have taken our educating and advice and moved well beyond us. All have tax-advantaged investments, real estate, stocks, funds, business interests. They are learning and enjoying it. Plus they have 30+ years to grow."

"I paid for night classes on investing at the university extension course for myself and my wife, and also for my son and son-in-law. I still encourage them to maintain regular saving, taking advantage of Roth IRAs, and 401(k)s, and not to use credit cards without paying off the balance."

"We taught our son about investing at an early age. We gave him a book called *Investing for Young People*. This book clearly described the importance of starting to save very early and compounding. At age 25, he has a 401(k), a pension plan where he is vested, six to seven years of IRA contributions, and a business on the side of his full-time job. He is also in the process of buying a townhouse. I think he listened and watched."

> "We encouraged our adult daughter to invest in Vanguard funds and to maximize her 403(b) investment. We encouraged her to invest in a Roth IRA. She is a very busy schoolteacher; however, we have encouraged her to review her holdings on a regular basis. We made GE stock gifts to two teenage grandsons and established educational IRAs. We established a computer accounting procedure so that each grandchild can track the performance of investments."

Sometimes the lessons don't stick, simply because nothing in the children's experience has convinced them that saving and investing are necessary undertakings. Sometimes the lessons lead in unexpected directions. "We encouraged our three children to learn to handle money. One child actually bought stock with lawn-mowing money at age 10. He was bored with the slow progress of Boeing, Nordstrom, and Weyerhaeuser and bought an engagement ring at age 23. He became an accountant." In the case of friends and spouses, those with no interest in investing may simply lack whatever combination of chemistry and experience it is that compels people to set aside something for the future.

> "Other relatives want to know how I retired so young (47), but eyes glaze over when I talk about saving more and spending less. They would rather I told them about a hot stock that will double overnight."

> "Some family members have their own methods. Others just aren't interested or would prefer that 'daddy do it.'"

> "I tried to interest children by giving them $10,000 when they graduated. They did not listen and spent it within a year. I would recommend giving stock, not cash."

> "I haven't had much luck. Subject seems to bore them."

A few "What Works" investors cautioned against discussing investments with friends or family members (though no one advised against doing so with their own children). Some people believe that investing is a private matter. Others would feel responsible if they shared investment advice that led to poor results.

> "Don't mix family and money."

> "I feel it's strictly a personal matter. Others have tried to interest me, and I walk away every time."

> "I do not feel competent enough to teach or advise others. When I did this in the past, I regretted the decision if the investment resulted in a loss."

> "It's difficult to advise when markets are falling. Some depend on me for advice, maybe too much."

> "My sister invested in a conservative mutual fund, but it is losing money just like the rest of us. Very discouraging for a new investor, especially since she is low income to begin with."

> "I do not want to be responsible for family members' or friends' investment decisions."

The tough stock markets since March 2000 have no doubt discouraged many tutors and pupils. Generally, however, frustrated tutor-respondents and those who refrained from discussing investments with family and friends were in the minority. A majority of respondents seemed to take satisfaction and pride in their efforts to help their children or other family members acquire tools for financial self-reliance. Whether or not these individuals leave a financial estate to their heirs or charity, they'll have established a powerful investment legacy.

Estate Planning

The "What Works" respondents didn't share much insight on estate planning, nor did we expect them to. Estate planning is a thicket of legal and tax-planning issues. A single mistake can jeopardize the chance that your estate will be managed according to your wishes. Planning also encompasses highly personal issues, such as the selection of guardians for minor children or decisions on how you should be cared for when you can no longer care for yourself. Although it's impossible to offer general advice about estate planning, this chapter contains a brief overview of some of the major tools used in estate planning, followed by a model plan for a hypothetical investor, based on the average "What Works" investor.

Your Needs and the Right Tools

Traditional estate planning involves preparing a will, creating trusts, naming beneficiaries for insurance policies and retirement accounts, selecting guardians for minor children, and many other tasks. In addition, some families need to address estate *tax* planning. Failure to plan for taxes could leave your family's property vulnerable to the federal estate tax, which can be levied at rates as high as 49%, and/or the generation-skipping transfer tax, also with rates as high as 49%. Rates are scheduled to decline to zero from now until 2010, but in the meantime, these taxes can be significant. Most states also impose some form of estate or inheritance tax.

Your estate includes just about everything you own—your investments, home, cars, insurance proceeds, jewelry, collectibles—everything. Add up your 401(k) plan, your home, and your other assets, and you might be surprised to find yourself confronting tax and planning issues once thought the domain of the superrich.

The basic estate-planning tools include the following:

- *Last will and testament*—Written instructions on how and when your assets are to be distributed. A will names an executor to oversee the distribution of your assets during probate—the legal process of settling an estate. A will is also used to create personal trusts. The most important nonfinancial reason for creating a will is to name a guardian for any minor children. If you don't have a will, a state court may dictate who will become guardian of your children. Your last will and testament, surprisingly, isn't always the last word on how your property is distributed. Property held in a trust is distributed according to the terms of the trust. Any assets held in insurance contracts, retirement accounts, or other contracts like annuities are distributed to beneficiaries named when you establish those accounts. (You can generally change the beneficiaries at any time.)

- *Personal trusts*—A legal arrangement through which property is held by a trustee on behalf of a beneficiary. The two main categories of trusts are those created when the trust creator is alive and those established upon his or her death. Revocable trusts are created while you're alive. They can be changed or revoked at any time. When you die, the trust generally becomes irrevocable. Irrevocable trusts can be created while you're alive or through the terms of a will or other personal trust after you die. Once established, an irrevocable trust cannot be revoked and generally cannot be changed unless you reserve that power to someone else. Some irrevocable trusts provide tax benefits that aren't available through any type of revocable trust. Trusts are often used to minimize or eliminate estate taxes, but they are also useful if:
  - You or a family member will need professional asset management in the event of incapacity or for some other reason.
  - Probate costs and hassles are so onerous in your state that they should be avoided.
  - You own property in more than one state.
  - You want to control how your beneficiary uses the money.
  - You have minor children or children with special needs.

Other Tools

In addition to a will and trusts, some estates include these other estate-planning tools:

- Advance directive for health care. Often called a living will, this document provides instructions to your physician on types of life-sustaining treatment you do and do not want if you can't make your own decisions.
- Health care power of attorney. Enables a trusted relative or friend to make decisions about your medical care if you are unable to do so.
- Financial power of attorney. Arranges for the handling of your affairs and management of your assets if you can no longer do so.

An estate plan may also include some elements not mentioned here. An estate-planning professional can help you create a plan that's right for your unique circumstances.

Your Tax-Planning Goals

Estate planning can become devilishly complex as your assets grow to more than $1 million (currently, the level at which federal estate taxes kick in). Families with estates worth more than $1 million can generally be divided into three tiers, according to their level of assets, to determine which estate-tax-planning strategies they should consider, as shown in Table 10.3. In all cases, it's wise to enlist the help of an estate-planning adviser or attorney to learn more about the different strategies and whether they're right for you.

Families in the first tier—estates valued at $1 million to $2 million—should use a basic strategy, making sure to take advantage of what the law provides, such as tax credits. A family in the second tier (a net worth of $2 million to $5 million) should be more aggressive, trying to freeze its estate at its current level and shift appreciation to the next generation. A family in the third tier (more than $5 million) might be more aggressive still and actively try to reduce the value of its estate.

TABLE 10.3 Tax-Planning Tiers

	Size of estate	*Sample techniques**
Tier 1: Basic	$1 million to $2 million	• Credit-shelter or bypass trusts. • Life-insurance trusts. • Modest tax-free gift giving. • Marital trusts.
Tier 2: Freeze estate	$2 million to $5 million	The above, plus: • Maximize tax-free gift giving. • Conservative estate-freezing strategies, such as grantor-retained annuity trusts and intrafamily sales and loans. • Charitable lead trusts.
Tier 3: Reduce estate	More than $5 million	The above, plus: • Generation-skipping transfer tax trusts. • Private annuities. • Aggressive estate-reduction strategies, such as limited partnerships and restricted management accounts. • Taxable gifts.

Source: The Vanguard Group, Inc.

*Ask your estate-planning advisers what techniques might be best for you. This is only a small sampling of the tools used in estate-tax planning; there are many varieties and alternatives.

The average high-net-worth investor in our "What Works" survey had an investment portfolio worth a little more than $2 million. For illustrative purposes, assume that these assets are owned by both husband and wife, and that the rest of the property (homes, life insurance, and so on) is worth $1 million, putting the value of their taxable estate at $3 million. (In reality, this estimate is probably low.) The couple meets with an estate-planning adviser, who recommends that their wills include directives to establish a credit-shelter trust (which allows a married couple to make full use of their combined estate-tax-exclusion amount, while benefiting the surviving spouse and ultimately passing the assets to the couple's children or other designated beneficiaries) on the death of the first spouse. To explain why, the adviser diagrams what could happen with and without a trust (Table 10.4). In the absence of a credit-shelter trust, the $460,000 that this couple may have wished to leave to their children and other beneficiaries makes its way to the U.S. Department of the Treasury. But a little planning—and the comparatively modest cost of professional advice—helps the heirs save a bundle.

Hire a Pro

The federal laws affecting estates changed dramatically in 2001 and will continue to change each year through 2011. You need a plan that's flexible enough to fulfill your wishes both now and as the rules change.

TABLE 10.4 What a Difference a Trust Makes!

	With a credit-shelter trust	*Without a credit-shelter trust*
Combined estate	$3 million	$3 million
First spouse dies in 2004 (law protects up to $1.5 million from estate tax)	• $1.5 million to credit-shelter trust • $1.5 million to marital trust controlled by surviving spouse	$3 million to surviving spouse
Surviving spouse dies in 2006 (law protects up to $2 million from estate tax)	No estate tax due	Estate tax of $460,000 due on $1 million

Source: The Vanguard Group, Inc.

This is one task you don't want to tackle on your own. Families often use a team of experts to develop an estate plan, perhaps including a financial planner or investment manager, a trust officer, an insurance agent, and an accountant. Eventually, you'll need a lawyer who practices estate law to draw up the documents. Obviously, the smaller your estate and the simpler your needs, the less professional help you'll require. Perhaps you simply need a will and a few other documents that can be prepared at a lawyer's office in a matter of hours.

Tomorrow's Legacy Is Yesterday's

Some "What Works" investors have already made arrangements for the management of their estates. Some may never need to tangle with the tax and legal complexities faced by those with substantial assets. But almost all of the people we heard from had given some thought to the behavioral legacy that their saving and investment practices leave to their children and others. They've also considered their financial legacies, of course, and some have made explicit goals of leaving money to their heirs and charities.

Earlier in this chapter, some of the investors described their efforts to give their family and friends the tools necessary to provide for their own financial futures. Not surprisingly, these investors were themselves the beneficiaries of an older generation's tutelage.

> "My mother realized it was important that young women have some experience managing money. When I was 14 or so, she started me on a monthly allowance, and I had to make my money last for the month. When you're 14, a month is a long time, so I had to think about saving."

> "My mother is the greatest investor that I admire. She taught me to put money away for the future, and it has paid off for me."

"My worst experience was the crash of '87. I asked my dad how the decline had affected him. He replied, 'They are still paying dividends, aren't they?' I learned if you pay cash, not borrowed money, for a stock, and it pays an acceptable dividend, you can weather almost any storm in the investment world."

"I admire the way my late husband began investing early, planning for retirement. He chose that we live a more modest lifestyle all along so that we would have few worries later on. He always said he wanted to be able to 'sleep well at night' rather than worry about an exorbitant mortgage or risky investments. I regret that he is not here to see the fruits of his planning."

"My grandfather, born during the Civil War, taught me the value of frugality and saving and about the miracle of compounding interest. Grandfather did not accumulate a lot of money, but following his simple principles, he traveled and lived comfortably during the Great Depression. Many of his contemporaries were on relief, or today's welfare."

The role of family and friends in the lives of these investors, as well as their thoughts about financial legacies, may prove useful to consider as you pursue your own investment plan. If you reach a point at which you'd like to spread the investing word, or contemplate a charitable gift, their experiences can provide guidance.

In the next chapter, our investors delve into a subject with little direct application to portfolio management but important implications for investment success: the traits that separate those who reach their goals from those who don't. This theme surfaces throughout *Wealth of Experience*, but in the next chapter the investors tackle the question head on. They also discuss attitudes toward money and investing that have helped sustain their long-term plans.

Planning Yields a Big Payoff

by Jack Brod

Jack Brod, a principal, directs Vanguard's Asset Management and Trust Services, which provides ongoing investment management and trust and estate-planning services for clients with significant investable assets. Mr. Brod, a Certified Financial Planner, joined Vanguard in 1995.

Estate planning doesn't have to be complex. Most decisions aren't irrevocable. And in my experience, estate planning has one of the highest payoffs in financial planning. Aside from all the money your estate can save in taxes, the value of just getting it right is one of the great "returns on investment" in financial planning. You can see the tremendous relief in clients' eyes. They say, "I feel really good that I've taken care of it." It's a responsibility, and there's peace of mind in knowing that you've done things the right way, and that your estate will be settled according to your wishes.

Even smart people make mistakes. I work with a family that holds a concentrated position in one stock. One of their goals is to minimize their exposure to this holding, but from self-admitted inattentiveness, they've typically given cash, rather than securities, to a charitable endowment. They've said, "Yes, I know that it's a good idea to give the stock, but I just haven't gotten around to it." You need to sit down and make a conscious plan so that everything happens according to your intentions.

Simple Mechanics, Difficult Issues

Because people are uncomfortable dealing with their own mortality, dealing with estate planning is something most people keep putting off. There are different philosophies. Some clients want to leave their heirs *X* dollars—no more, no less. We also have what I call "last dollar, last breath" clients who would like to spend their last dollar as they take their last breath. But for every one of these clients, there are three or four who haven't given it any thought. Some people never get around to it, and the decisions are made for them—and their heirs—by the courts.

Although the technical end of estate planning can be relatively simple and inexpensive, the process can raise difficult issues. Some people wrestle with leaving money to their kids versus charities. Another big issue is how much is enough? Parents want their kids to have incentives and a certain work ethic, so they may try to structure their estates to encourage their children to reach goals. At the same time, many appreciate that their children may have values or goals different from their own. For most parents, the bottom line is to do something good, without creating negative consequences. As you accumulate assets, it's important to consider your financial legacy, because the decisions you make now can have implications down the road.

Following Through: An Adviser Can Help

A lack of follow-through is also common. It's not just getting the documents right; you may need to change the title of some assets or make other arrangements. A good lawyer and adviser can make sure you follow through on all the steps that come after the documents are drawn up.

Estate planning is really a process, not a one-time event. Your plan is based on premises that may or may not change, so it's a good idea to revisit and revalidate your plan every few years. In this decade, the big uncertainty is taxes. Federal estate taxes are being phased out through 2010, but as the law currently stands, they'll be reinstated in 2011. People who set up their plans three to five years ago need to revisit them, and then revisit them again in another three to five years.

An effective adviser plays a consultative role. When you work with hundreds of people, you see many of the same issues again and again. You get a sense of what needs to be done to move the process along. One thing to be wary of, however, is product-driven advice—or advice that steers you to buy certain products. Insurance, for example, is often oversold as an estate-planning tool. It has its place—in closely held businesses without a lot of liquidity, or when the estate will need a cash infusion when a person dies—but it's oversold. There are scores of insurance agents out there who call themselves estate planners, and not surprisingly, life insurance is always a central part of the solutions they devise.

The Bigger Picture

I liked the "What Works" investors' emphasis on their behavioral legacies, the lessons and values they want to leave their heirs. It's not all about leaving tangible assets. Estate planning is really about transferring values, both tangible and intangible.

My view is that you want to start by teaching children or other beneficiaries about the fundamentals of saving and investing: Live within your means, use time to exploit the miracle of compounding, diversify. Take a building-block approach. Teach people these concepts before you teach them about investment products. I'm not a big fan of giving young children individual stocks. That confers financial benefits, but you miss the building blocks. I like the approach taken by Laurel Murphy, the woman who taught her sons about saving. If your children can learn these fundamentals, the investing part will come easily when they're responsible for their own financial security.

Action Steps

Donald P. DiCarlo, Jr., is Vanguard's director of trust and estate planning. His ten reflections on estate planning summarize the steps to take and issues to consider as you plan your estate.

1. Seek to convey your values as well as your assets.
2. Consider and plan for the attributes and circumstances of those who will benefit from your estate as carefully as you consider and plan for what they will receive.
3. Clearly articulate your goals, or they will probably not be achieved.
4. Do not assume that the federal estate tax has or will be permanently repealed or that death-related taxes will not be a significant burden. These taxes can often be reduced or eliminated with the use of common estate-planning strategies.
5. Be sure that the risks, costs, and complexity of a proposed estate plan are suitable for you and balanced against your objectives.
6. Select fiduciaries who are trustworthy and competent and who share or are willing to promote your personal values.
7. Understand that estate planning is a process, not an event, and that the objectives of an otherwise sound estate plan are likely to be frustrated if the plan isn't properly implemented.
8. Understand that a prudent investment methodology is critical in achieving estate-planning goals.
9. Be sure that the products and services being offered by a financial adviser or institution are *serving* your estate plan, not *driving* it.

10. Understand that your adviser's role in the estate-planning process should be one of facilitator and consultant, not of decision-maker. It is your attorney's role to create the plan and draft the documents.

chapter eleven

ADOPT PRODUCTIVE HABITS AND ATTITUDES

The experiences of the "What Works" investors have made plain that the *mechanics* of investing are not complicated. It's relatively easy to develop an investment plan, select an asset allocation to help you meet your goals, and implement it with suitable investment instruments. Indeed, our respondents have offered advice on each of these tasks.

> ***The* mechanics *of investing are not complicated. . . . However, the* practice *and* discipline *of investing, through good times and bad, are emotionally and intellectually demanding.***

However, the *practice* and *discipline* of investing, through good times and bad, are emotionally and intellectually demanding. In Chapter 6, "What Works" respondents discussed some of the emotional sandbags that can knock an investment plan off track. Yes, it's easy to know what you should do, but hard to do it. Do people with certain temperaments and habits of mind stand a better chance of success in their pursuit of long-term goals?

In this chapter, the "What Works" respondents identify the traits of successful—and unsuccessful—investors. Although some of these traits seem to be intrinsic to people's personalities, many can be cultivated by people who, for example, aren't naturally patient. The "What Works" investors also share some philosophical observations about the role of investing in their lives. Their insights may strike a chord and offer perspective that can help you approach investing more productively.

Traits of Successful Investors . . .

Our survey respondents offered two primary schools of thought on the traits of successful investors. Most investors said that success was the result of discipline and emotional fortitude. A smaller group said that success reflected superior intellect and investing knowledge. The minority viewpoint seems to be widely held by the public at large. To read most financial publications, or even to sit in front of financial television for a few minutes, is to conclude that success demands a razor-sharp mind and laser-like focus.

> "Successful investors pay virtually daily attention to portfolio, business conditions, and investment climate."

> "These investors have knowledge of the market and world events' effects on it."

> "Successful investors have outstanding knowledge of stocks, bonds, and other financial instruments. Operate within the bounds of your tolerance level, invest for a long time frame, beware of fads, never get in a position where you must sell a stock, and develop an understanding of how political and social activities will affect individual stocks."

> "A keen interest. A large investment of time."

"In addition to research, successful investors have an understanding of how the pieces fit together. The most successful are far ahead of the rest on this."

Perhaps the ability to evaluate the impact of geopolitical developments on your portfolio can enhance your returns. Perhaps not. What's unequivocally true is that this kind of intense physical and intellectual effort is not necessary for success. People often seem to assume that the traits of successful investors are much like the traits of successful professionals in other fields. You wouldn't want to see a doctor who doesn't keep abreast of new treatments. You wouldn't want to hire a computer programmer who hadn't upgraded his skills in the past few years. You wouldn't want to be represented by a lawyer who hasn't practiced law since the 1960s. However, for reasons that have preoccupied academics for more than half a century, eagle-eyed attention to the markets and corporate financial statements isn't a prerequisite for investment success.

On balance, the "What Works" investors believed that success depends more on qualities that make up your temperament than on your intellect and education or earning power. Indeed, 18% of the high-net-worth investors in our survey never graduated from college (though 49% pursued study beyond college). And as noted in Chapter 1, 16% of the high-net-worth respondents who are still in the work force had household incomes of less than $100,000 a year. That's a relatively comfortable threshold, of course, but the figure suggests that the accumulation of significant wealth doesn't demand an equally significant income. Many successful investors say they aren't geniuses, just disciplined and patient.

Consider some of the following practices and characteristics that our respondents identified as the traits of successful investors.

"Discipline. Routine. Going for singles and doubles rather than grand slams. Patience."

"A nonemotional view of when to sell, or buy for that matter. Investing in things they know. A willingness to take risk."

"Successful investors have a strategy and stick with it. A successful long-term strategy accounts for market ups and downs, and successful investors resist the temptation to deviate from their plan."

"Realistic expectations, consistent approach, steel nerves."

"Luck, patience, and a steady cash flow sufficient to cover day-to-day costs of living."

"Ability to live happily below your means."

"Successful investors are not impulsive, not greedy. They are giving, have a plan, have some knowledge of investing, even if it's only general knowledge. They enjoy investing, and they are willing to take prudent risks."

"Discipline. Courage. Patience. Common sense."

"Making a plan and sticking by it. Don't think you can change every time the market hiccups and be a good investor. While I think I'm a middle-of-the-road investor, I will take a chance sometimes on something that hits my fancy, but I recognize that I might just be throwing that money out the window."

"Successful investors are patient. They are realistic, not greedy. They save rather than spend. They try to read a lot to keep informed, but are very skeptical."

"Successful investors become interested in investing at an early age. They are patient. They don't become greedy. They pay attention to their portfolio at least annually. They set up regular savings habits. They maximize tax-deferred accounts."

"Successful investors are knowledgeable and informed. Awareness of your own priorities and needs is crucial. Be realistic about risk, and allocate investments for balance."

"I think successful investors are analytical. They study and learn from experience. Even your mistakes are helpful if you learn from them."

. . . And the Unsuccessful Investors

Our investors also identified traits common to unsuccessful investors—in many cases habits and practices that they wrestled with in their own experience.

"Unsuccessful investors lose track of their goals. They get caught up in the moment. They become emotional."

"Unsuccessful investors are looking for the fast bucks, rather than allowing for growth over a longer period of time."

"Impatience and greed to get rich quickly. Risky investments aren't much different than gambling. Of course, buying high (when everyone is excited) and selling low (when you are discouraged about lack of increase in values)."

"Unsuccessful investors try to time the market, which is extremely hard, and you must do it twice, getting in and getting out, and then do it over and over again."

"Unsuccessful investors get new cars, boats, vacation tours, credit-card debt."

Investment Attitudes

Vanguard asked investors about their views on certain investing attitudes. Table 11.1 presents the attitudes that received the strongest agreement and those that received the weakest. (A similar table appears in Chapter 1, detailing the differences between "early" and "later" savers.) It's not surprising, yet it is noteworthy, that these respondents who, on average, have been investing for some 35 years, overseeing portfolios worth $1.8 million, have a very positive attitude toward investing. Only 2% of the "What Works" investors agreed completely that they'd "rather spend today than save for the future," whereas 39% said that they "get a lot of satisfaction from saving for the future."

It's impossible to know whether the "What Works" investors started with positive attitudes or developed them over time, but their positive cast of mind clearly makes it easier to establish and stick with a long-term investment plan.

TABLE 11.1 Attitudes About Investing (Percentage of 'What Works' respondents who 'agreed completely')

	Total (%)	*Core (%)*	*High-net-worth (%)*
Financial success enables me to have freedom and independence to live my life as I desire.	51	37	54
I get a lot of satisfaction from saving for the future.	39	35	41
I enjoy managing my money.	37	33	38
I don't like dealing with money and finances.	3	3	3
It's pointless to plan for retirement, it's too far away.	2	2	2
I'd rather spend today than save for the future.	2	1	2

Source: The Vanguard Group, Inc.

Philosophy—Investing in Life

One conclusion reached by the "What Works" investors was that long experience in the investment markets can make you philosophical. Certainties never come to pass. Your fail-safe plan fails. And as much as you can enhance your prospects with good habits and a steadfast emotional approach, some people concluded that success still depends, at least a little bit, on luck. Others thought that a successful approach to the markets' unpredictability included humility and a sense of humor.

A few investors drew connections between lessons learned in the capital markets and the principles they followed in other areas of their lives.

Investment Philosophy: The Big Picture

For some people, a successful investment program reflects the principles that guide them in other areas of their lives. An unsuccessful program is at odds with those beliefs. This relationship was especially clear in the comments of Mel Hawthorne, a semi-retired respondent from New York.

"The worst experience I had was trying to time the market with aggressive stocks recommended by a broker who wanted to churn my account. I don't own individual stocks any longer. That was not a game I wanted to play. It was too great an investment of costs, and time, and emotional energy. There was a period in New York in the 1970s, I would have been in my thirties at that point, when it was an all-encompassing activity. The roller-coaster ride was initially fun. Every day, I was checking stocks, calling brokers; I was reading too much about stocks. My main interests were in nonprofits and church, but that's not how I was allocating my time. I was happier as a person if I had a simpler life.

"*Simpler* to me means I don't have my money spread everywhere. It's diversified, but not spread across 40 or 50 funds at different companies. I've consolidated most of what I have at Vanguard. That's one kind of simplification for me. Another sort of simplification is, I believe in maintaining what you have, starting with your body. So you eat well, keep your doctor's appointments, and so on. When it comes to what you own—your car, your house, your clothes—do the little repairs early, so you don't have to pay someone to come in later to do the big repairs. So you don't need to buy a new car every two or three years. Eliminate clutter. I've never been one to collect things, though that's not to say I don't have those inclinations. You don't own a lot of things that need to be replaced.

"I want my life to be my focus. I want the financial aspect of it to be a supplement, an enabler for the interests that I have. So I don't want to be really rich, but I don't want to be really poor. I always tell my friends that I don't want to be old and poor. Being poor is OK when you're young and a student, and there's a certain amount of creativity in that, but I don't want to be old and poor.

"The overall lesson is that each of us has to determine how much time and attention we want to give to the investing part of our lives. It varies for every individual. More than a risk tolerance, it's a time or commitment or attention tolerance, or a focus tolerance. To go from the daily management of the portfolio to a more relaxed, sort of a monthly management of the portfolio . . . that was the biggest thing for me to accomplish. It wasn't good for me to tend to it daily: I was making bad decisions, I was worried, I learned greed and fear. And I didn't like either of those to be so primary in my life. To get away from that, I think, was life-changing for me."

"Money creates freedom. The desire for freedom easily outweighs the short-term pain of not having."

"It is better to be lucky than smart."

"Everyone falls prey to mistakes and gains from some luck."

"My most successful investment comes from my good luck."

"Well, when you get up to be about my age, you realize that investment and monetary things are only so important. You can't take it with you. I don't think my father-in-law ever learned that."

"Successful investors know what they don't know (which increases as I get more knowledge, experience, and maturity)."

Investor Traits and Your Portfolio

The investors' observations about the traits that lead to success, as well as their more philosophical reflections on the markets, suggest that it's wise to develop an investment approach that complements your temperament. Doing so seems to be the best way to steady your emotional rudder and stay engaged with a process that lasts a lifetime. Of course, just about every successful approach will include some mix of stocks, bonds, cash, and maybe real estate or other investment assets. Every successful plan also includes a strong savings component and an ability to fight counterproductive impulses. But as you put the pieces together, it makes sense to develop a plan that accounts for your unique personality and temperament.

Through their survey responses and conversations with Vanguard, the "What Works" investors imparted what for many was a lifetime of investing wisdom and advice. In the concluding chapter, we offer some final words from the respondents and summarize the key habits and practices that can help you reach your financial goals.

Successful Investing: The Long Term Is Key

by James H. Gately

James H. Gately is managing director of Investment Products and Services at Vanguard, overseeing Vanguard Brokerage Services®, annuities and insurance, financial planning, and asset management and trust services for high-net-worth clients. Mr. Gately, a Chartered Financial Analyst, joined Vanguard in 1989.

The first thing to note about the successful investors I've met and worked with is that they come in all sizes and shapes, from all professions and backgrounds, and from all stages of life. The cross-section of our Flagship™ shareholders (with Vanguard assets of at least $1 million) is truly amazing. Some have advanced degrees; some never went to college. Some are successful in professions such as law or medicine; others are small-business owners. Some work with advisers, some without. No one could walk into a room and pick out the successful investors.

A Focus on the Long Term

One thing these successful investors generally have in common, however, is that they don't get carried away by the issues of the day. They don't ask us many questions about whether Alan Greenspan [chairman of the Federal Reserve Board] will cut interest rates and what that will mean for the stock market. They don't wonder what tension in the Middle East will mean for their portfolios. The headlines aren't driving their decisions.

Their questions are much more fundamental or philosophical. At a meeting with Flagship clients, for example, we might be asked, "You're offering a lot of new services. Will that raise fund expense ratios?" (the answer is no), or financial-planning questions, such as whether international stocks can diversify a portfolio (the answer is yes). It's clear that these clients are thinking several years ahead, not about what's going to happen in 2003.

Unsuccessful investors, however, are just the opposite. They get caught up in the moment and have a tendency to chase performance. Once a year, I see a friend who hasn't enjoyed as much investment success as he could have. He always asks me about the current "hot fund." I can predict what he's going to ask about by looking at a table of 12-month trailing returns. In 2002, it was Vanguard® GNMA Fund, which soared as stocks sank. The year before it was something else, and next year it will be something else still.

Humility and Attention to Risk

Clients who have enjoyed notable investment success also tend to be pretty humble about their ability to outsmart the next guy. They've come to the conclusion that the market is pretty wise. Many of them have had adverse experiences, and they'll say, "How could I have been so dumb as to take that risk?" So there's a surprising degree of humility among people who have achieved notable financial success.

They also think about risk as much as they do about return. In our conversations with these clients, they're always trying to ferret out what could go wrong with a fund or an investment strategy. They have faith in the ability of our economic system and market to generate wealth, and they combine that faith with healthy skepticism about investment management.

The Illiquidity Trap

For some reason, unsuccessful investors, particularly those who earn high incomes, often fall into the trap of investing in illiquid assets. There's a psychology that says if you can't measure an investment's price on a daily basis—as you can with a stock, bond, or mutual fund—you can assume it's doing better. At my 2001 college reunion, a classmate and his wife told me that because their stocks and funds were down, they were going to invest in hedge funds. I asked them about the funds' strategies. They weren't really sure, but they'd heard that all the good mutual fund managers were going to hedge funds, so they were going to follow the "smart money." Finally, the woman said, "You work in this industry. Do you give advice?" I said, "Yes. Be careful." And she said, "That's it?" And I said, "If you're going into hedge funds, be careful."

Over time, illiquid investments have come and gone. Many "What Works" investors talked about their bad experiences with investing in illiquid limited partnerships in real estate and oil during the 1970s and 1980s. In a sense, those partnerships were the hedge funds of their day.

Successful investors take a disciplined, long-term approach to investing using liquid financial assets, which are much easier to understand than illiquid assets, less costly, and, generally, much less risky.

Action Steps

- Think long term; successful investing is a process that takes decades, not months.
- Consider risk as well as return. Sooner or later, risk comes to the surface. Don't be taken by surprise.
- Be wary of illiquid investments, especially those you don't understand.

chapter twelve

FOLLOW THE EIGHT COMMANDMENTS

The "What Works" investors are men and women, working and retired, young and old, from all walks of life. On average, they've enjoyed financial success, but the group also includes people whose investment programs have been derailed, at least temporarily, by decisions that have been more educational than remunerative.

What unites the "What Works" investors is that at some point, they began to save and invest, learning valuable lessons along the way. Their approaches are by no means the same. Some respondents are diehard stockpickers. Others are big believers in the talents of select mutual fund managers. Some invest only in broadly diversified, low-cost index funds. Whatever the details of their strategies, successful investors have a few principles in common.

The Eight 'What Works' Commandments

Investing is a lifelong journey. You may march from the purchase of a home, to paying for the education of a child, to financing your retirement—to whatever objectives are dictated by your unique circumstances. The experiences of the "What Works" investors suggest that by observing eight simple commandments, you can stay on the straight and narrow as you pursue your financial goals.

1. **Save.** Saving is the bedrock of a successful investment program, but it's a step many Americans just don't manage to take. For some people, saving is a natural inclination, but most have to work at it. Once the habit is ingrained in your budget (and mind), however, saving can be relatively painless. The "What Works" investors offered a number of tips that helped them to follow this imperative.
2. **Plan.** An investment program can be successful (or unsuccessful) only in the context of an investment plan. The plan can be as simple as "save enough for retirement by contributing to my 401(k) plan," as many investors said. With time and experience, you can refine your plan, including guidelines about target rates of return, asset allocation, investment selection, estate planning for your heirs, and so on. Make a plan, and you'll approach the task of investing with a sense of purpose and greater confidence.
3. **Learn.** The "What Works" investors indicated that most people can acquire the knowledge and skills to be successful investors through a combination of study and experience. Others work with a trusted professional. Whichever path you choose, these investors suggested that you spend some time learning the basics.
4. **Diversify and allocate.** Investors' greatest disappointments (and successes, for that matter) resulted from a failure to diversify. A technology fund blew up, jeopardizing their nest egg. A one-time blue chip went bad, destroying their investment. A concentrated bet can make you rich, of course, and has done so for some of these investors. For most of us, though, the risks of concentrated holdings are too high. For the same reason that they didn't invest their retirement money in a single lottery, the "What Works" investors were strong advocates of diversification. They also championed the related, and equally important, concept of asset allocation. Your mix of stocks, bonds, and cash determines both

the returns you earn and the risks you experience. Successful investing means finding the right balance of risk and return.

5. **Keep emotion in check.** Fear and greed are the culprits behind many of the worst investment decisions. The financial markets provoke strong emotional responses that can undermine a sensible, long-term investment plan. Media commentary and news about the markets can be a major distraction. Our investors offered a number of tips, both tactical and psychological, for keeping emotion out of your investment program.
6. **Monitor.** You don't need to obsess about your portfolio. In fact, that kind of intense focus is usually counterproductive. From time to time, however, it's sensible to assess the progress of your investment program and rebalance your holdings to match your target asset allocation. There are both simple and complex methods for monitoring your holdings, depending on the investments you select.
7. **Keep your costs down.** Low costs are the most reliable predictor of high returns. Everyone wants high returns. Fewer people pay attention to costs. Magazines and newspapers run lists of the highest returns for the quarter or year, not the funds with the lowest costs. The "What Works" investors have discovered that cost and return are inextricably linked, a fact that big institutional investors have long understood. Our respondents suggested strategies for maximizing your investment returns by keeping costs to a minimum.
8. **Be smart about taxes.** Your goal should be to maximize your after-tax returns, not to minimize your taxes. That simple principle can help you avoid many of the pitfalls identified by "What Works" investors. After all, it's not what you pay in taxes, it's what you have left that's vital. It's smarter to earn $10 and write a $4 check to the tax collectors than to earn $5 tax-free.

These eight commandments can help you reach your investment goals. As your investing journey unfolds, you'll encounter additional investment-related considerations—the planning of your estate, for example, or the desire to equip others with the knowledge and skills to meet their own financial responsibilities. "What Works" investors have wrestled with these challenges, too, and their experiences may illuminate a path that's right for you.

Battle-Tested Counsel

The "What Works" survey was conducted during the longest and deepest stock market downturn since the Great Depression. From March 2000 through the end of December 2002, the broad U.S. stock market declined more than 40%, destroying some $7 trillion in stock market wealth. The news contained shocking reports about ethical lapses and outright fraud at high-profile companies. "What Works" investors felt the pain, and it was clear that the confidence of some was badly shaken. "With the present rash of corporate scandals involving stock prices being manipulated by crooked accounting so that insiders could make big profits on their stock options, I have some concerns about whether the small investor has an honest chance to make a profit in the stock market," said one respondent. "These crimes certainly make the idea of an efficient market seem an academic idealization, especially for those whose pension savings were locked into the stocks of their corrupt corporations."

A Pennsylvania investor in his late fifties who worried about having enough assets for retirement said, "I think that the markets are limited by the integrity of those who run the companies. We are now experiencing the residue of the 1960s, when values like integrity, honesty, and forthrightness were trashed."

The grueling downturn no doubt disappointed all stock market participants. The best that can be said for this period is that it reinforced principles cast aside during the giddy stock markets of the late 1990s. As one investor put it, "Although I knew the market couldn't continue to grow as it had in the 1990s, and knew a diversified portfolio, while less glamorous than a growth portfolio, was my ultimate objective, I didn't proceed as such. I thought dollar-cost averaging and money market cash would protect me from a market downturn. I ignored bonds, and I planned to reallocate when I retired (January 2001)."

What is striking about the investors who shared their wisdom here is how little the bear market changed their investment approach. On balance, these investors didn't abandon the principles they had followed throughout their investment lives, either before the stock market's run-up or during its precipitous fall. Some of them had learned to stay the course as a result of the brutal downturn in stocks and bonds from 1973 to 1974 and the stock market's stunning 1987 collapse. They kept a focus on the long term.

> "Stay invested. Eventually the market will come back. I'm not in this alone."

> "In the financial world, the good and the bad go in cycles. Good times are not available forever."

> "I still feel optimistic, but I'm also trying not to think about my plummeting portfolio too much. I'm banking on recovery."

> "Given the current market environment, the smartest thing we have done is own stock and bond mutual funds and individual bonds."

> "Accept the fact that markets go down as well as up. Stay the course."

> "Stay on track. We will not stop investing completely just because the market has not been doing well. We understand the concept of dollar-cost averaging. During the bull market, we bought shares at very high valuations. At present, we have cut our investments a little bit because we're able to buy a lot of shares at lower prices."

The eight commandments culled from the "What Works" investors' experience are durable, tested in good markets and bad. These simple principles can help you to survive the tough times while positioning you to profit from the better times to come. "My best experience was weathering the bear market of 1969 to 1983," said a "What Works" respondent, referring to a period when the stock market's returns barely outpaced inflation. "Lesson: It pays to be persistent and not give up."

That was good advice for the 20th century. It will be just as good in the 21st.

Thanks!

The "What Works" investors showed that real people can develop successful investment programs without access to highly paid advisers or complicated investment strategies. These people have made mistakes, of course, which often yielded some of the most valuable lessons in this book. But the "What Works" investors have also shown that if you follow a few simple principles, the inevitable mistakes will pale in importance beside the successes.

It should go without saying, of course, that The Vanguard Group, and anyone who has been inspired by these accounts to start, or improve, an investment program, owes the "What Works" investors a debt of gratitude for sharing their experiences with us.

NOTES

Chapter 1

1. Steven F. Venti and David A. Wise, *Choice, Chance, and Wealth Dispersion at Retirement*, Working Paper 7521 (Cambridge, Mass.: National Bureau of Economic Research, February 2000).
2. Ibid.
3. Roger Lowenstein, *Buffett: The Making of an American Capitalist* (New York: Random House, 1995), 34.
4. "Top Ten," *Forbes 400: The Richest People in America*, September 30, 2002: 102.

Chapter 2

1. Venti and Wise, *Choice, Chance, and Wealth Dispersion at Retirement*, 55 (Table 9).

Chapter 3

1. Stanley O'Neal, quoted in Suzanna Wooley with Amy Feldman, "A New Bull at Merrill Lynch," *Money* 31(3) (2002): 89.

Chapter 4

1. Source for 1999: Securities Industry Association. Estimate for 1980 households: The Vanguard Group, Inc.
2. Based on 1,280.7 million shares outstanding at the end of McDonald's fiscal year 2001. Cited in McDonald's Corporation, *2001 Summary Annual Report* (Oak Brook, Ill.: McDonald's, 2002).

Chapter 5

1. *U.S. Mutual Fund Fact Book,* 2002 ed. (Washington, D.C.: Investment Company Institute, 2002), 61.
2. Federal Reserve Board, *Flow of Funds Accounts of the United States: Flows and Outstandings* (Washington, D.C.: Board of Governors of the Federal Reserve System, December 7, 2001).
3. Ibid.
4. Ibid.
5. Burton G. Malkiel, *A Random Walk Down Wall Street*, 6th ed. (New York: W.W. Norton & Co., 1996).
6. William J. Bernstein, www.efficientfrontier.com, 2002.
7. Mark M. Carhart, "On Persistence in Mutual Fund Performance," *Journal of Finance* 52(1) (March 1997): 57–82.

Chapter 6

1. Malkiel, unpublished research, cited in "Investing for the Future: Don't Fixate on the Past," *In The Vanguard* (The Vanguard Group) (Summer 2001): 6.
2. Brad Barber and Terrance Odean, "Trading Is Hazardous to Your Wealth: The Common Stock Investment Performance of Individual Investors," *Journal of Finance* (April 2000): 773–806.
3. A. Tversky and D. Kahneman, "Advances in Prospect Theory: Cumulative Representation of Uncertainty," *Journal of Risk and Uncertainty* 5 (1992): 279–323.
4. Daniel Kahneman, quoted in Jason Zweig, "Do You Sabotage Yourself? *Money* (May 2001): 78.
5. Ibid.
6. Scott Burns, "Revising the Couch Potato Portfolio," *Dallas Morning News*, September 30, 2002; www.dallasnews.com/business/scottburns/couchpotato/columns/stories/060902dnbizburns.7271a628.html.

Chapter 7

1. *How America Saves: A Report on Vanguard Defined Contribution Plans* (Valley Forge, Pa.: The Vanguard Group, September 2002), 47.

Chapter 8

1. Mark C. Carhart, "On Persistence in Mutual Fund Performance," *Journal of Finance* 52(1) (March 1997): 57–82.
2. Scott Cooley, "Fish in the Low-Cost Pond," *Morningstar Mutual Funds*, March 6, 2002: S1.
3. Ibid., S2.

Chapter 10

1. Investment Company Institute, *2001 Profile of Mutual Fund Shareholders*, ICI Research Series (Washington, D.C.: ICI, 2001), 6.
2. Employee Benefit Research Institute, *Parents, Youth & Money Survey* (Washington, D.C.: EBRI, 2001), 1.
3. Ibid., 11.

GLOSSARY

The "What Works" investors and Vanguard officers use many of the following terms in *Wealth of Experience*. You'll encounter much of this jargon as you develop your own investment program, but it's unlikely that you'll need to be fluent in highly specialized terms, such as *information ratio*. Still, they're defined here just in case the need arises.

active management

An investment strategy that tries to beat the returns of the financial markets. Active managers rely on research, market forecasts, and their own judgment and experience in making investment decisions. You choose active managers in the hope of outpacing the market, but it's important to know that the odds are against you. The opposite of active management is *passive management*.

adviser

An individual who provides investment advice. In the mutual fund industry, the individuals or organizations that manage a fund's portfolio are called *investment advisers*. Investment professionals who help you develop an investment program may also be called investment advisers.

alternative investments

Assets other than the traditional, liquid (readily bought and sold) asset classes—common stocks, bonds, and cash. Examples of alternative investments include real estate as well as highly specialized vehicles, such as leveraged buyout funds, venture capital funds, hedge funds, private equity, and distressed-debt funds.

annuity (variable, fixed, and immediate-fixed)

An *annuity* is a contract between an individual and an insurance company. An annuity is also the only product that gives an individual the option to receive a guaranteed (subject to the claims-paying ability of the insurer) stream of income designed to last for an entire lifetime. This income stream is usually set up at retirement. The principal kinds of annuities are variable, fixed, and immediate-fixed.

- Variable annuity—A tax-deferred investment that is much like a mutual fund, but with an insurance "wrapper." The value of the investment fluctuates in line with the performance of the portfolios (stocks, bonds, and cash) within the annuity. Investors in variable annuities typically are guaranteed that they'll receive at least the amount they invested, thanks to a contract that insures their initial investment.
- Fixed annuity—Tax-deferred investments that typically guarantee a fixed rate of interest over a given period of time.
- Immediate-fixed annuity—A contract purchased with a lump sum that guarantees you a given income over a period of time or over your lifetime. These contracts are typically purchased with after-tax dollars.

asset allocation

The process of deciding how your investment dollars will be split among various classes of financial assets, such as stocks, bonds, and cash investments.

asset classes

Major categories of financial assets, or securities. The three primary classes are common stocks, bonds, and cash investments.

back-end load

A sales commission paid when the investor sells mutual fund shares. May also be called a *contingent deferred sales charge*. Some funds gradually phase out back-end loads for investors who stay in a fund for several years. See also *front-end load*.

benchmark

See *index*.

bid–ask spread

The *bid* is the current price at which investors can sell shares, while the *ask* is the current price at which investors can buy shares. The difference between the two is commonly referred to as the *spread*. For securities that trade infrequently, this spread can be equal to several percentage points of the security's value.

blue chips

Stocks issued by large, established companies that boast significant financial resources and often pay dividends. According to the Oxford English Dictionary, the term is derived from the highly valued blue chips used in gambling. Although there is general consensus on which companies make up the market's blue chips, the term is subjective. For example, some investors might argue that Dell Computer, one of the market's largest and most profitable companies, is not a blue chip because it operates in the fast-changing technology sector and doesn't pay a dividend.

bonds

An IOU issued by corporations, governments, or government agencies. The issuer makes regular interest payments on the bond and promises to pay back your "loan" at a specified point in the future, called the *maturity date*.

capital gains distribution

A fund's payment to mutual fund shareholders of gains (profits) realized on the sale of securities. Capital gains are distributed on a net basis, after the fund subtracts any capital losses for the year. When gains exceed losses, you—the fund investor—owe taxes on your share of the gain, unless those shares are held in a tax-sheltered account such as an IRA or 401(k) plan. When losses exceed gains for a year, the fund carries the difference forward to offset future gains.

cash investments

Investments in interest-bearing bank deposits, money market instruments, and U.S. Treasury bills or notes. These are conservative, short-term investments, typically with maturities of 90 days or less.

certificates of deposit (CDs)

CDs are interest-bearing bank deposits that require the depositor to keep the money invested for a specific period of time. They are federally insured for up to $100,000 per bank, per account registration. Although often purchased through banks, CDs are also available through brokers.

compounding

The growth that you get if you reinvest your investment income and gains instead of taking the cash. First, you earn money on your investment; then, you earn money on your original investment plus the amount you earned.

contingent deferred sales charge

See *back-end load.*

credit risk

The chance that the issuer of a bond will fail to pay interest or to repay the original principal on time—or at all. Every bond is subject to credit risk, but some issuers are extremely safe (U.S. Treasury and government agencies), some are typically safe (large, financially sound companies with good track records), and some can be downright dangerous (small, young companies with shaky finances). The greater the credit risk, the higher the interest rate, or *yield*, a bond should pay.

day-trader

A creature of the late 1990s bull market who traded in and out of stocks rapidly, often holding no position for longer than one day, in an attempt to parlay incremental gains on many positions into sizable aggregate winnings. This species has been approaching extinction since the bursting of the stock market bubble.

diversification

Spreading your money among different classes of financial assets and among the securities of many issuers. Diversification is sometimes called a free lunch, because by combining different securities with different patterns of return, you can reduce a portfolio's risk without a commensurate decline in its potential return.

dividend

A fund's payment of income to mutual fund shareholders from interest or dividends generated by the fund's investments. Also, cash payments to owners of common stock, paid out of a company's profits.

dollar-cost averaging

Investing equal amounts of money at regular intervals on an ongoing basis. This technique reduces risk of loss from a sudden market downturn and reduces the average cost of shares over time, since you acquire more shares when prices are lower and fewer shares when prices are higher.

duration

A way to gauge how much the price of a bond or bond fund will go up or down when interest rates fluctuate. A fund with an average duration of 10 years will see its price drop about 10% with every 1 percentage point increase in market interest rates; the price would rise 10% if interest rates fell 1 percentage point. A bond fund with a duration of 2 years would see its share price rise or fall about 2% in response to a 1 percentage point decrease or increase in interest rates. In short, the longer the duration, the bigger the price change for a bond fund or bond when interest rates rise or fall.

equity

Equity means ownership, whether in a home or business. Stocks are often called equities because they represent ownership in a company. Entrepreneurs and business owners often refer to the value created in their businesses through years of hard work as sweat equity.

exchange-traded funds (ETFs)

A hybrid investment that combines the diversification benefits of mutual funds with the trading flexibility and continual pricing of individual securities. Like stocks, ETFs are traded on an exchange and can be bought and sold at intraday prices through a brokerage account, rather than at end-of-day prices. Like mutual funds, most ETFs are registered investment companies that offer diversification and professional management. The ETFs created so far use indexing as an investment strategy.

expense ratio

The percentage of a fund's average net assets used to pay annual fund expenses. The expense ratio takes into account costs such as management fees, legal and administrative outlays, and any 12b-1 marketing fees.

front-end load

A sales commission, or load, that you pay when you buy shares of a mutual fund. For example, if you invest $3,000 in a fund with a front-end load of 4%, you'll start off with an account balance of $2,880.

guaranteed investment contract (GIC)

An investment typically offered in group retirement plans that pays a specified rate of return for a specific period of time.

high-yield bond

A bond (or an IOU) issued by a company or a government with a low credit rating. Also known as *junk* bonds. High-yield bonds exemplify a key trade-off in investing: Higher-risk investments offer the potential for greater reward. Companies with iffy prospects must pay higher rates of interest to entice investors to lend them money.

income

Interest and dividends earned on securities held by a mutual fund. These earnings are paid to fund shareholders in the form of income dividends. The fund shareholders then owe taxes on this income, unless the fund is held in a tax-sheltered account, such as an IRA or 401(k).

income risk

The possibility that the income stream you're receiving from a mutual fund or other investment will decline. This risk is most acute with money market funds and other short-term investments. If interest rates fall, short-term investments quickly reflect the new rates, and the income you were getting from your money market fund drops.

index

A statistical benchmark that's used to measure the performance of the stock or bond markets—or particular parts of those markets. They are standards against which investors can measure the performance of their investment portfolios.

index fund

A mutual fund that seeks to track the performance of a market benchmark, or index.

individual retirement account (IRA)

A tax-advantaged way to save for retirement. If you have earned income from a job, you can put money in IRA accounts for yourself and for your spouse, if the spouse does not work outside the home. Investment earnings within a *traditional IRA* are not taxed until withdrawn from the account, and the money you put into the account can be deducted from taxes, if you qualify under the rules. With a *Roth IRA*, you don't get an up-front tax deduction, but the earnings on the account may be withdrawn tax-free (under certain conditions, of course). Withdrawals from an IRA made before age 59½ may be subject to a 10% federal penalty tax.

inflation

A general rise in the prices of goods and services. This is a big concern for investors—especially those with long-term goals—because the amount you're investing and earning will lose purchasing power as inflation rises. The higher the rate of inflation, the more you'll have to invest or earn to stay ahead. Over decades, inflation can end up confiscating a significant chunk of your assets.

inflation-protected securities

A special type of bond whose principal value changes to reflect changes in the level of consumer prices. These securities sound more complex than they actually are. The key thing to know is that the principal value and, therefore, the interest income of the bond goes up with inflation.

information ratio

A statistical measure used to determine a portfolio manager's risk-adjusted returns. It is calculated as a manager's return in excess of a benchmark's returns divided by the manager's tracking error relative to the benchmark. Tracking error (the difference between the return of a portfolio and its benchmark) is defined as the standard deviation of excess returns.

initial public offering (IPO)

A company's first sale of equity shares in the public stock markets. A company sells shares to investors to raise money for investments or other business purposes.

interest rate risk

The risk that a bond or bond fund will decline in price because of a rise in market interest rates. Prices move in the opposite direction from interest rates. If you own a bond that pays 5% in annual interest and new bonds coming onto the market pay 6%, the market value of your bond would fall to reflect the fact that higher-yielding bonds are available.

investment horizon

The length of time you expect to keep a sum of money invested. Many of your financial decisions will hinge on the answer to the question: When will you need the money?

load fund

A mutual fund that charges a sales commission, or load. These commissions can be as high as 9% of the amount you invest.

low-load fund

A mutual fund that charges a sales commission equal to 3% or less of the amount invested.

management fee

The fee paid by a mutual fund to its investment adviser. The fee may be based on a percentage of assets, and it may vary depending on how the fund performs relative to a market benchmark. This fee is part of a fund's expenses, which are taken out before you earn anything from the fund.

market capitalization

What a company is worth in the stock market. Market capitalization equals a stock's share price multiplied by the number of shares outstanding. For a stock mutual fund, market capitalization is determined by the market caps of the securities it owns. It's important to know whether a fund focuses on large-, mid-, or small-caps—or on companies of all sizes—so that you can build a diversified portfolio and also so that you can be sure that you're comparing your fund's performance against a relevant benchmark or competitive group.

market risk

The possibility that an investment will fall in value because of a general decline in financial markets. This is one risk you can't avoid, no matter how much you diversify. When the broad stock market slumps, so will a well-diversified stock portfolio.

money market fund

A mutual fund that seeks to maintain a stable share price and to earn current income by investing in interest-bearing instruments with short-term (usually 90 days or less) maturities. Money market funds are not insured by the federal government, but if you put $1 into the fund, you can reasonably expect to get $1 out, plus interest.

municipal bonds

See *tax-exempt bonds*.

mutual fund

An investment company that pools money from individuals and uses it to buy securities such as stocks, bonds, and money market instruments.

net asset value (NAV)

The market value of a mutual fund's total assets, less its liabilities, divided by the number of shares outstanding. It's commonly known as a fund's share price.

no-load fund

A mutual fund that does not charge a commission on purchases or sales. Like load funds, no-load funds incur operating expenses, but you incur no charge to buy or sell the shares of no-load funds.

options

A contract between two investors, a buyer and a seller. The buyer (option holder) pays a premium for the right (but not the obligation) to buy or sell securities at a specified price by a set date. The seller (or option writer) receives the premium and is obligated to deliver or buy the securities if the buyer exercises the option. Options can be appropriate in special situations. Investors with large holdings in a single stock, for example, may be able to protect significant gains with option-based strategies. And employees who receive stock options as compensation become options investors by default. But as speculative vehicles, options can be very dangerous because they give you the ability to make big bets on the moves in a security's price without putting up much capital. It's easy to get in over your head.

passive management

Also known as *indexing*. A low-cost investment strategy that seeks to match, rather than outperform, the return and risk characteristics of an index by holding all, or a statistically representative sample, of the securities that make up the index.

portfolio

For you, it's all the investments you own; for a fund, it's all the securities it holds.

principal

The amount of money you put into an investment. This term also refers to the face value of a bond and to the amount still owed on a loan, like your home mortgage loan.

prospectus

A legal document that provides detailed information about a mutual fund, including discussions of the fund's investment objectives and policies, risks, costs, past performance, and other useful information.

R-squared

A statistical measure of the degree to which an investment's past returns are correlated with the past returns of a benchmark. An R-squared of 1.00 means that a fund's returns are synchronized with the benchmark's returns. An R-squared of 0 indicates that the fund's pattern of returns bears no resemblance to that of the benchmark's returns.

redemption fee

A fee that you may be charged for selling shares in certain funds. When a redemption fee is paid to the fund management company, it's a back-end sales load, or commission, and can fairly be considered an undesirable toll. However, some redemption fees are actually good for long-term investors—they're paid to the fund, not the management company, to compensate all fund shareholders for the costs of buying and selling securities and to discourage short-term traders.

stocks

Securities that represent part-ownership in a company. Each share of stock is a claim on a proportion of the corporation's assets and profits, some of which may be paid out as dividends.

tax-exempt bonds

Also known as *municipal bonds*, or *muni bonds*. Typically, you won't pay federal income tax on interest you receive from an investment in bonds issued by municipal, county, and state governments and agencies. If you buy bonds issued by municipalities in the state where you live, you're off the hook on state and local income taxes too.

total return

The percentage change, over a given period, in the value of an investment, including any income paid on it. Total returns reported for a mutual fund take into account the effect of fund expenses and assume that income dividends and/or capital gains distributions are reinvested. This is the best measure of mutual fund performance over time.

tracking error

The difference between the returns of a portfolio and the returns of the benchmark that it seeks to track. The term is most often associated with indexing, where tracking error is a measure of the index fund manager's skill at matching the index's returns.

turnover rate

A measure of a mutual fund's trading activity, the turnover rate can affect a fund's tax efficiency. A turnover rate of 50% means that, during a year, a fund has sold and replaced securities with a value equal to 50% of its average net assets.

volatility

The fluctuations in market value or returns of a mutual fund or other security. The greater a fund's volatility, the wider the spread between its high and low prices.

yield

The rate at which an investment earns income, expressed as a percentage of the investment's current price. Yield is what you get paid for owning a fixed income investment, such as a money market fund, a bond fund, or a bank certificate of deposit. Stocks that pay dividends to investors also have yields—the annual amount of the dividend, divided by the stock's price.

INDEX

P

Q

R